AIRLINE WITHOUT A PILOT

LESSONS IN LEADERSHIP

Copyright/Disclaimer

Dedication/Acknowledgment

I dedicate this book to the thousands of loyal, professional Delta Air Lines employees who have persevered in keeping a fine company together, even during times when there was questionable top leadership.

This book is also dedicated to the memory of my Mother and Father—Sarah Austell and Lee Nolan. They were both quiet but shining examples of a deep, abiding faith in God; a life of substance and meaning; servant leadership; and behavior driven by a heart full of love. I often thank my Maker for blessing me with such fine parents. Dad's gentle, kind manner combined with a unique strength of character. Mother's commitment to me manifested itself in many ways. She was a great teacher who modeled for me the importance of living a life of integrity. She also was the catalyst for my love of learning and appreciation of the value of the written word. Their spirit lives on with me. I pray it will be reflected on each reader of this book.

Acknowledgments

I am grateful for the many friends and family members who have encouraged me while I researched and wrote this book. Particularly I appreciate the time of the 59 "Delta family" members I interviewed and their willingness to share candidly experiences, information and knowledge about the company and its people.

Thanks also to my clients at Management Advisory Services, Inc. during the past 23 years. Our work together taught me many important leadership lessons; key ones are shared in the book.

About Harry Nolan

Harry Nolan has been a top management consultant to major U.S. and international corporations for over 20 years. He provides highly successful business and leadership strategies to clients of his firm.

The following client comments reflect their appreciation for the high value of his work to their organization:

"Thank you for all the hard work and excellent results you have accomplished over the last 6 months for us. Your enthusiasm and determination to succeed were inspiring both to my team and me. You tackled enormous projects including our pricing strategy and Internet strategy. Your work was extremely valuable as you helped us through a difficult transition period."

Odie C. Donald, CEO
Cable & Wireless CAI
(now lead Director of Fortune 500 company)

"Harry Nolan and Management Advisory Services, Inc. have had an important, long-term impact on our company. His advice has been instrumental in helping us achieve substantial sales growth over the last 10 years and increased profitability in an industry where sales have been stagnant."

Paul A. Guden, CEO
H.A. Guden & Co., Inc.

"You have made a significant difference to me, my management team and the employees of the company as we have gone through a period of major transition."

David G. Dahm, President & CEO
LeasePlan USA

"Thank you for all the help you gave me and my team when I was CEO at Logistics Health before I decided to open my own venture capital firm. During the many months we worked together, I learned to value your considerable business knowledge, diagnostic ability, insight into people, practical approach and professional and personal integrity. You were valuable in many ways. For example, the strategic planning retreat you helped me plan and then ran for the management team was the most effective planning session of the many in which I have participated in different companies through the years. I would not hesitate to recommend you to anyone needing a seasoned, effective management consultant who is the rare combination of a strategic thinker and one who knows how to implement strategy."

David J. Cook, CEO
Logistics Health, Inc.
(now Managing General Partner
DJC Holdings LLLP)

"You have consistently given the company team and me valuable advice that has been useful in a highly competitive environment."

William H. Brown, President & CEO
Heely-Brown Company

"Your work has been very valuable to us. You have helped focus our Executive Management Team in developing objectives, strategies and related action plans to insure our strategies get implemented as we planned. The accountability and time lines you insisted be part of our plans have helped us in carrying out our plans effectively. I have been impressed with the employee feedback you generated and the strategic recommendations you generated as a result of this feedback. This feedback has helped me and the Executive Management Team identify and address issues that may not have been identified otherwise. It has also helped us in the business integration process over the last several years, blending two companies with significantly different cultures, policies and procedures. Finally, you have helped me create a more effective department. Your work has been instrumental in helping integrate two geographically and culturally different groups into a focused, functioning team."

Mary Elizabeth Christy
Senior VP / Human Resources
LeasePlan USA

"Thank you again for the exceptional professional assistance you have provided me, my management team and the university. Having retained you based on your expertise and prior experience in effectively assisting enterprises with strategic planning and the strategic planning process, your superb professional reputation was confirmed throughout our engagement. You immeasurably assisted in the development and refinement of our new and evolving vision and strategic plan."

Dr. Betty L. Siegel, President
Kennesaw State University

Table of Contents

PROLOGUE ....- 1 -

    WHY THIS BOOK WAS WRITTEN ....- 1 -

    TIMELESS LEADERSHIP LESSONS.................................- 1 -

    DELTA AIR LINES – A LEADERSHIP STORY.......................- 2 -

    DELTA'S TURMOIL...- 2 -

    LEADERSHIP'S ROLE IN THE TURMOIL..........................- 4 -

    IN 1978, A RISKY BUSINESS GOT RISKIER ....- 5 -

    LOW COST AIR CARRIERS EMERGE AND PROSPER..................- 7 -

    VALUJET / AIRTRAN ....- 8 -

    COMMERCIAL AVIATION FINANCIAL CROSSROADS ....- 9 -

    FOCUS ON DELTA'S BOARD AND CEO ....- 10 -

    COMPREHENSIVE, HUMAN STORY ....- 11 -

INTRODUCTION ....- 13 -

    THE AUTHOR AND THE BOOK ....- 13 -

        Author's credentials to write this book...........- 13 -

        How the book was researched.......................- 14 -

    OVERVIEW ....- 18 -

    DELTA'S SIX 9/11'S ....- 20 -

    THE ROLE OF THE BOARD OF DIRECTORS ....- 21 -

        Board's expanded role in CEO selection ....- 22 -

        Board's expanded role in management consulting....- 22 -

    THE HORSE AND THE DITCH ....- 22 -

        Leadership keeps the horse out of the ditch.......- 22 -

        Delta now and Delta's future ....- 23 -

1 –LEADERSHIP ....- 25 -

    LEADERSHIP MODELS ....- 25 -

PRINCIPLES OF LEADERSHIP ....- 26 -
A BOARD'S TOP TASK IS CHOOSING THE RIGHT LEADER ....- 28 -
CHANGING RELATIONSHIP BETWEEN CEOs AND BOARDS .....- 32 -
THE DECLINE OF 'ROCK STAR' CEOs...................................- 33 -
BOARDROOM CULTURE CHANGES TO SKEPTICISM ....- 34 -
PERSONAL FINANCIAL LIABILITY OF BOARD MEMBERS ....- 34 -
PUBLIC ACCOUNTING FIRMS NO LONGER ICONS ....- 35 -
NEWS MEDIA NO LONGER GET A FREE PASS ....- 36 -
MANDATORY FOR BOARDS TO STEP TO THE PLATE................- 36 -

2 – CULTURE ....- 37 -

CULTURE AND ACQUISITIONS ....- 37 -
HOW CULTURE DEVELOPS...- 38 -
CULTURE AND THE LEADER ....- 39 -
CULTURE AND THE ROLE OF THE BOARD ....- 41 -

3 – BIRTH – TEENAGE YEARS.......................................- 43 -

HOW DELTA STARTED ....- 43 -
THE LONG SHADOW OF ONE MAN ....- 43 -
TRUE LEADERSHIP ....- 44 -
LEADERSHIP VACUUM ....- 45 -
WOOLMAN'S SIMPLE BUSINESS FORMULA ....- 45 -
    Integrity .... - 46 -
    Customer service .... - 46 -
    Teamwork .... - 46 -
    Family... - 47 -
    Safety .... - 47 -
    Heart.. - 48 -
    Stewardship .... - 49 -
    Cost control .... - 50 -
    Financial sense .... - 51 -
WOOLMAN'S MANAGEMENT STYLE ....- 52 -
    Servant leadership .... - 52 -
    Accessibility.. - 52 -
    Treating employees with value, dignity and respect ...... - 53 -
    Management by walking around.................................. - 53 -

Humility .... - 55 -
Hands on management .... - 55 -
Private Employee Assistance Program .... - 56 -
Warm heart and tough love .... - 57 -
THE "DELTA FAMILY" WAS AND IS A REALITY ...... - 58 -
DELTA EXPERIENCES ITS FIRST 9/11 .... - 59 -

4 – EARLY ADULT– MATURITY .... **- 61 -**

WOOLMAN-TRAINED DELTA EMPLOYEES CARRY ON .... - 61 -
3 CEOS HELP DELTA REACH MATURITY .... - 62 -
WOOLMAN INFLUENCED DOLSON AND GARRETT .... - 62 -
Dolson CEO from 1966- 1971 .... - 62 -
Beebe CEO from 1971 - 1978 .... - 63 -
Beebe sets stage for protégé Allen to become CEO .... - 65 -
Garrett CEO from 1978 - 1987 .... - 66 -
"WE LOVE TO FLY AND IT SHOWS" CAMPAIGN .... - 67 -
TV COMMERCIALS USING DELTA EMPLOYEES .... - 68 -
WOOLMAN-TRAINED CFO .... - 69 -
IMPRESSIVE FINANCIAL RESULTS .... - 70 -
DELTA'S 2ND 9/11 - DEREGULATION .... - 70 -
WOOLMAN SHADOW DIMS BUT SURVIVES .... - 71 -

5 – DELTA'S MIDLIFE CRISIS .... **- 73 -**

HOW RON ALLEN BECAME CEO .... - 73 -
NOTABLE QUOTES .... - 73 -
DELTA'S 3RD 9/11 – ALLEN NOT A CAPTAIN .... - 73 -
CHOICE OF THE BOSS IS NOT A SUCCESSION PLAN .... - 75 -
SUCCESSION PLANNING THE PROPER WAY .... - 75 -
VIABLE CEO CANDIDATES PASSED OVER .... - 76 -
PERCEPTIONS OF RON ALLEN .... - 78 -
LEADER TEMPERAMENT: BOARD RESPONSIBILITY .... - 81 -
RON ALLEN'S AMORPHOUS GOALS .... - 82 -
PURCHASE OF PAN AM ASSETS .... - 83 -
Pros and cons of Pan Am asset purchase .... - 84 -
Too little due diligence and too high a price .... - 84 -
Known Pan Am maintenance problems ignored .... - 85 -

Predictable Pan Am maintenance problems happened .. - 85 -

Pan Am facilities problems .... - 86 -

LEADERSHIP 7.5 – CONTRACT WITH EMPLOYEES IS BROKEN . - 87 -

Goal never achieved but profitability returned .... - 87 -

Two part contract is broken .... - 88 -

Manner of employee cuts hurt morale .... - 89 -

Restructures du jour and programs du jour begin .... - 90 -

Consultant's cookie cutter approach foundation of 7.5 .. - 91 -

Consultant X gets an annuity .... - 95 -

POST EVALUATION OF LEADERSHIP 7.5 .... - 96 -

Positive effects of 7.5 .... - 97 -

Lessons learned .... - 97 -

Specific regrets about 7.5 .... - 99 -

EMPLOYEE SURVEY DOCUMENTS THE 7.5 DAMAGE .... - 99 -

FINANCIAL RESULTS UNDER ALLEN .... - 102 -

ALLEN'S DEPARTURE PERFORMANCE .... - 103 -

ALLEN'S LUCRATIVE DEPARTURE .... - 104 -

ASSESSMENT OF ALLEN .... - 105 -

6 – OUT-OF-BODY EXPERIENCE .... - 109 -

LAME DUCK CEO CREATES PRESSURE ON BOARD .... - 109 -

DELTA BOARD DECIDES TO FIND CEO OUTSIDE .... - 109 -

NOTABLE QUOTES .... - 110 -

MULLIN HIRE – DELTA'S FOURTH 9/11 .... - 110 -

IN GENETICS AND CEOS OUTCROSS MUST IMPROVE SPECIES - 111 -

MULLIN CREDENTIALS: LOW CHANCE FOR CEO SUCCESS ..... - 112 -

MULLIN'S BEST FRIEND WAS RON ALLEN .... - 114 -

MULLIN STARTS OFF ON RIGHT FOOT .... - 115 -

MULLIN'S TRUE COLORS START SHOWING EARLY .... - 115 -

FAVORABLE RESULTS ON 1998 EMPLOYEE SURVEY .... - 116 -

MULLIN'S PRESCRIPTIONS MAKE PATIENT SICK .... - 117 -

INTERNAL PROBLEMS OVERSHADOW EXTERNAL .... - 117 -

MULLIN'S INITIAL STEPS .... - 118 -

MULLIN'S NEW TEAM BEGINS DELTA'S FALL .... - 119 -

ARROGANT NEWCOMERS WITH CONTEMPT FOR DELTA .... - 119 -

ARROGANT ATTITUDES PRODUCE ARROGANT BEHAVIOR ..... - 120 -

COMMON SENSE AND PEOPLE SKILLS SCARCE .... - 121 -
WATCH WHAT I SAY, NOT WHAT I DO .... - 122 -
REVOLVING DOOR FOR MULLIN CFO'S .... - 122 -
QUESTIONS ABOUT DELTA'S PENSION PLAN INVESTMENTS . - 124 -
MULLIN ABDICATES DELTA FOR WASHINGTON .... - 125 -
REACTION TO MULLIN'S WASHINGTON FOCUS .... - 126 -
BEGINNING OF THE END FOR MULLIN TEAM .... - 127 -
EXECUTIVE COMPENSATION FIASCO .... - 127 -
DELTA BOARD SWEETENS EXECUTIVES' PIE .... - 129 -
EXECUTIVE COMPENSATION FIASCO COVER-UP .... - 130 -
REID INTERVIEW WHEN COVER-UP BEGAN .... - 131 -
ENTIRE "DELTA FAMILY" SUFFERS EXCEPT EXECUTIVES ..... - 133 -
SECRECY VEIL OFF EXECUTIVE COMPENSATION FIASCO ..... - 135 -
EXECUTIVE RETENTION SCHEME DOESN'T RETAIN .... - 136 -
MULLIN LOSES ABILITY TO LEAD/BOARD LETS HIM STAY ... - 137 -
MULLIN ALLOWED TO HANG ON/CARTY OUT IMMEDIATELY - 139 -
INEFFECTIVE DAMAGE CONTROL/NON-APOLOGIES .... - 141 -
MULLIN FACES THE INEVITABLE / ALLOWED TO RESIGN ...... - 141 -
GRINSTEIN'S PHILOSOPHICAL 'APOLOGY' .... - 142 -
FINANCIAL RESULTS DOCUMENT DESTRUCTION TO DELTA . - 143 -
MULLIN'S AMAZING STATEMENTS AT THE END .... - 147 -
MULLIN AND TEAM NOW FLY FIRST CLASS FREE ON DELTA - 149 -
MULLIN LEAVES BEHIND MESS/WALKS OUT WITH MILLIONS - 150 -

7 – DELTA'S FIGHT FOR SURVIVAL .... - 151 -

GRINSTEIN STEPS TO THE PLATE .... - 151 -
GRINSTEIN'S REFRESHING APPROACH .... - 152 -
WHO IS GERALD GRINSTEIN? .... - 153 -
GRINSTEIN WALKS TALK/SHARES PAIN WITH EMPLOYEES ... - 153 -
GRINSTEIN'S WORK ETHIC .... - 154 -
GRINSTEIN SENDS A FRUGALITY MESSAGE .... - 155 -
GRINSTEIN HONORS DELTA'S TRADITIONS .... - 155 -
GRINSTEIN THE PERSON .... - 156 -
PERCEPTIONS OF GRINSTEIN .... - 156 -
GRINSTEIN'S FIRST 18 MONTHS A FINANCIAL DISASTER ...... - 156 -
DELTA'S 6TH 9/11 .... - 157 -

FOUNDATION FOR BANKRUPTCY LAID LONG AGO .... - 158 -
LEADERSHIP PRODUCED THE BANKRUPTCY .... - 159 -
BLAMING EXTERNAL FACTORS IS AN EXCUSE .... - 160 -
GRINSTEIN A CONUNDRUM .... - 161 -
GRINSTEIN'S RESPONSIBILITY FOR DELTA'S CONDITION ..... - 162 -
DELTA'S EMPLOYEE PENSIONS A PRIORITY .... - 164 -
DELTA STOPS PENSION PLAN PAYMENTS .... - 166 -
ASKING CONGRESS FOR PENSION RELIEF .... - 167 -
ENGAGING LOYAL DELTA RETIREES .... - 170 -
2005 "THE YEAR OF DELTA'S PEOPLE" .... - 171 -
DELTA'S TRANSFORMATION PLAN .... - 172 -
KEY TRANSFORMATION PLAN ELEMENTS .... - 173 -
MAJOR HURDLES AHEAD .... - 177 -
IS AIRLINE INDUSTRY SUSTAINABLE AT $70+ OIL? .... - 178 -
IMPORTANCE OF FUEL HEDGING .... - 179 -
CAPITALIZATION AND ACCESS TO CAPITAL .... - 180 -
EMPLOYEES TAKING ANOTHER SALARY HIT........................ - 182 -
ASSESSMENT OF GRINSTEIN'S PERFORMANCE .... - 184 -

8 – DELTA'S BANKRUPTCY .... - 185 -

NOT SO FAST, JERRY .... - 185 -
EMERGING FROM BANKRUPTCY SUCCESSFULLY .... - 185 -
GRINSTEIN MUST STAY AS CEO.. - 186 -
GRINSTEIN HAS AN OBLIGATION TO STAY .... - 187 -
SELLING OUT DELTA IS NOT THE ANSWER .... - 188 -
LEADERSHIP, NOT FUEL, THE PROBLEM.............................. - 188 -
DELTA CAN ILL AFFORD ANOTHER ALLEN OR MULLIN .... - 189 -
QUALIFIED CANDIDATE AVAILABLE FOR COO .... - 191 -
PROTECT DELTA'S UNIQUE REMAINING ASSET .... - 192 -
UNIQUE ASSET ERODED AND FRAGILE BUT ALIVE .... - 194 -
CONTRAST BETWEEN DELTA AND NORTHWEST.................... - 195 -
CONTRAST BETWEEN DELTA AND AMERICAN .... - 195 -
RETAIN DELTA'S EMPLOYEE PENSION PLAN .... - 196 -
RENEW "SERVICE AND HOSPITALITY FROM THE HEART" ... - 197 -
REHIRE BBDO AS DELTA'S ADVERTISING AGENCY............. - 199 -
ELIMINATE HUMAN RESOURCES .... - 200 -

REPLACE HR WITH STRATEGIC CULTURE LEADER .... - 201 -

TURN LOOSE AND EMPOWER THE SIX SIGMA PEOPLE .... - 201 -

SIX SIGMA IS OFTEN MISUSED .... - 203 -

SIX SIGMA AT DELTA .... - 204 -

FIRE ALL THE MANAGEMENT CONSULTANTS .... - 206 -

DELTA UNABLE TO AFFORD MANAGEMENT CONSULTANTS . - 207 -

REQUIRE CEO AND BOARD APPROVE ANY CONSULTANTS ..... - 208 -

REPLACE CONSULTANTS WITH RETIRED EXECUTIVES .... - 209 -

THREE PART BANKRUPTCY STRATEGY .... - 211 -

RECOGNIZE INTERNATIONAL IS A SHORT-TERM FIX .... - 211 -

DEVELOP A REALISTIC BUSINESS MODEL FINALLY .... - 212 -

INSIST ON A SENSE OF URGENCY .... - 213 -

DELTA'S BOARD MUST STEP TO THE PLATE .... - 214 -

BOARD MUST ROLL UP THEIR SLEEVES AND WORK .... - 214 -

9 - LEADERSHIP LESSONS .... - 217 -

10 – EPILOGUE .... - 219 -

APPENDIX .... - 221 -

Letter 1 – Delta's Katrina response shows Delta's heart and spirit still alive even in bankruptcy .... - 221 -

Letter 2 – How Delta's leadership created the situation for which employees and retirees are now made to pay   - 228 -

Prologue

Why this book was written

A key purpose of this book is to provide significant lessons in leadership and a practical approach to apply these lessons.

The book was also written to help the thousands of "Delta family" members find answers to the question, "What happened to my company?"

It provides insights for the additional thousands not employed directly by Delta but whose livelihoods are directly or indirectly affected by it. As the largest employer in Georgia, Delta's condition has a broad effect on the economy of Atlanta, the state of Georgia and the entire region. It impacts thousands nationally.

For anyone interested in Delta, the book goes beyond the incessant, daily newspaper headlines to provide a fresh perspective on this unique institution.

Timeless leadership lessons

Examples are drawn from many different experiences. However, Delta Air Lines, Inc. was selected as the primary example of timeless leadership lessons. These lessons are very valuable without regard to Delta's future as a company.

These lessons come from an understanding of what made Delta successful and profitable for decades and then what brought this fine company to its knees.

In Delta, we have a dramatic example of the profound effect (positive and negative) a CEO and Board can have on a company and tens of thousands of people

– employees, their families, suppliers, governments and an entire region.

Delta, a respected member of the *Fortune* 500 for many years, was recently removed from the S&P 500 stock index since its stock value had dropped to single digits. On September 2, 2005, the price dropped below $1 in intraday trading. Following the bankruptcy filing, it now trades at less than $1 a share. Clearly, the company faces the prospect of delisting by the New York Stock Exchange. This would mark another major turning point in Delta's downward spiral.

Delta Air Lines – a leadership story

The title of the book, "Airline Without A Pilot", came about during a lengthy dinner discussion about leadership with a long time friend and retired CEO.

It captures the essence of the period in Delta's history when events and results demonstrate that Delta was without *an effective CEO* at the 'stick' of the company.

This recent period is directly contrasted to the decades when Delta did have an effective CEO.

Delta has always had good people throughout the organization – professionals who understand how to run a fine airline delivering customer service at a profit.

The key to its long, initial period of financial success, as well as what got Delta into its current mess, has been the top leadership.

Delta's turmoil

Many believe that the foundation of the problems actually began in 1978 after airline deregulation. However, management led the company to 12 years of sustained profitability immediately after the law was passed.

Delta's problems first surfaced publicly in the early 1990's coinciding with: a recession; higher fuel prices resulting from the first Gulf war; the purchase of selected assets – planes, routes and real estate - from Pan Am.

The four money-losing years between 1991 and 1994, under then CEO Ron Allen, saw a cumulative loss of $2.2 billion. As a result, Allen initiated a widespread cost reduction effort called "Leadership 7.5." This name came from the initiative's goal - to reduce the Cost Per Available Seat Mile (a common metric in commercial aviation for unit cost) to 7.5 cents.

Allen then returned Delta to profitability for three consecutive years between 1995 and 1997, with a cumulative profit of $2.7 billion. Allen was terminated as CEO by the Board of Directors effective June 30, 1997, the end of that fiscal year for the company.

Allen's successor as CEO, Leo Mullin, led Delta through three more years of profitability between 1998 and 2001.

In early 2001, well before 9/11/2001, the financials wheels had begun to come off under Mullin. During the 3 years between January 1, 2001 and the end of 2003, when he resigned as CEO, Delta lost a combined $3.3 *billion*. Mullin surpassed by $1.1 billion the cumulative losses during Allen's losing years.

The downward momentum under Mullin was so strong that in 2004, current CEO Gerald Grinstein's first year, Delta lost an additional $5.2 *billion*. In the first 6 months of 2005, Delta lost another $1.5 *billion*.

The cumulative loss of $10.0 *billion* during the last 4 ½ years has created turmoil. In addition, Delta has cut 23,000 jobs and cut the pay of all remaining employees. Management has announced more pay cuts and benefit cuts are coming soon. The turmoil will persist for the foreseeable future, particularly now that Delta has filed for bankruptcy.

Delta's shares traded as high as $71.56 in 1999 prior to the start of the losses that began under Mullin.

Delta's market capitalization had dropped to about $200 million by mid-August 2005. On September 26, 2005, it had dropped below $132 million. On that same day, the market capitalization of far smaller competitor AirTran was slightly over $1 billion.

Leadership's role in the turmoil

Much of this turmoil can be attributed to external factors – for example, 9/11/2001 and its aftermath; the growth of low cost airlines; skyrocketing fuel costs.

However, this book shows that leadership decisions are the prime cause of the turmoil. At every key juncture, it is clear that a wiser decision would have minimized or perhaps alleviated the effect of these external factors.

The leadership lessons from this unfortunate period for Delta are profound for those who wish to avoid a similar fate. They are as valuable, perhaps more so, than the leadership lessons from the earlier times of more successful Delta CEOs.

Prologue

In 1978, a risky business got riskier

The airline business has always been a tough one to manage.

Since its inception in the 1920's, commercial aviation has been risky. It is both capital and people intensive. The government regulations and rules have created a sometimes artificial or fluid context in which to operate a business.

Even after Congress passed a law deregulating the industry in 1978, the government still carries a big stick affecting the industry, particularly on safety issues.

The Airline Deregulation Act of 1978 changed the rules so that basically any airline can fly anywhere domestically they want at any price. Until that time the Federal government allocated routes to provide appropriate service to cities but protected the airlines from traditional competition.

The long-term, strategic effect of this law was to expose trunk carriers like Delta to potential significant price competition; it removed the assurance of limited route competition.

The Boards and management of legacy carriers, including Delta, have generally done a poor job of anticipating the predictable changes in the business and making the strategic shifts to deal profitably with these changes.

In general, management of those carriers continued to be operationally focused – which worked under regulation – instead of becoming marketing focused – that has been necessary to survive after deregulation.

They failed to heed the admonition that the rumbling in the distance was the buffalo coming.

The promise of President Jimmy Carter, who aggressively urged airline deregulation, was lower fares for customers and a stronger industry.

Some would argue the results have been disastrous, certainly for airline stockholders. In 1978 the 5 largest airlines in the U.S. (and the world, omitting Aeroflot) were United, American, Pan Am, TWA and Eastern. After 25 years of deregulation, 4 of the 5 have gone bankrupt; American has come close. U.S. Airways has gone bankrupt (twice in three years) and Continental at least twice. Now Delta and Northwest are on the list.

Noted aviation industry attorney Dean Booth has also observed that other airlines have indirectly or directly gone bankrupt, some after a merger first: National, Piedmont, Southern, Ozark, TransTexas, Braniff, Frontier, Mohawk and Allegheny.

The bottom line is that 22 of the 25 largest airlines at the time of Carter's deregulation have gone bankrupt.

Booth also makes a compelling case that no one can show how deregulation has been good for the consumer or businesses either.

First, comparing overall fares is nearly impossible, noting that on the same aircraft in 2002, the difference averaged 2,000 percent – someone on the same airplane going to the same destination paid 20 times as much as someone else. Second, Booth observes, "There won't be lower fares on non-existent carriers."

Booth predicts airline re-regulation.

Prologue

Low cost air carriers emerge and prosper

The new regulatory environment enabled smaller or new carriers to set up a point-to-point, low cost, low fare model in contrast to the legacy carriers' (including Delta) traditional hub-and-spoke model.

The poster child of low cost carriers is, of course, Southwest Airlines. Co-founded in 1967 by Herb Kelleher, now an airline legend, Southwest has grown steadily in 38 years to become a profitable, major player in the industry. It has also legitimized the low cost concept for others.

Since 1978, both start-up airlines as well as legacy carriers have introduced variants of the Southwest model.

In 1991, low cost carriers had approximately 4% of the commercial aviation market. Today low cost airlines have over 25% of the total domestic passenger traffic. This share is growing and is projected to be 40% by 2006.

The Federal government policy since the early 90's has been to encourage this low cost competition, particularly by pushing major airports to open up more gates and landing slots to them.

For years after deregulation, the legacy carriers like Delta discounted the long-term effect of low cost carriers. Without realizing it, they behaved like the proverbial frog in the kettle, who boiled to death while the water heated up slowly from room temperature.

In the early 90's, when the legacy carriers finally began to wake up to the potential threat, often their reaction was merely verbal acknowledgment in an annual report or half-hearted steps.

ValuJet / AirTran

In 1992, four former airline presidents created an upstart, low-cost carrier named ValuJet. The cheeky founders headquartered ValuJet in Atlanta and based it at Hartsfield (now Hartsfield-Jackson) International Airport where Delta enjoyed an 80% share of traffic.

Delta was unconcerned enough to sell ValuJet their used DC-9-30 aircraft. This plane was the initial backbone of the ValuJet fleet.

The airline launched service in October 1993. ValuJet was profitable from the start, even in the face of a strong competitive response from Delta.

The low fare, no reservations, no frills airline, with a zany cartoon airplane for a logo, clearly filled a need in the leisure market.

Many discounted the future of the startup, particularly over allegations of shoddy safety practices. When ValuJet Flight 592 crashed in the Florida Everglades, killing all 110 people on board, some said the inevitable had happened.

Shortly before that crash, I ignored cautions about ValuJet's safety and flew roundtrip between Atlanta and Jacksonville. On the flight down, a bathroom visit exposed an unattached metal toilet seat container. Had the aircraft hit rough air, the container had the potential of striking a passenger, seriously injuring or even decapitating them. Then the toilet seat would not stay up and had to be held with one hand, while the other hand was occupied. Finally, in an embarrassing but in retrospect humorous moment, the door unlocked and popped open on its own with passengers in line waiting to use the bathroom.

I convinced myself this was a rare occurrence. I overlooked it, along with the threadbare carpet and torn seats, because the $39 fare each way was so attractive.

However, the same thing happened on the return trip to Atlanta the next day in a bathroom on the other side of the plane. I have never flown that airline again.

ValuJet bought AirTran and assumed its name. Steadily increasing revenues and market share, as well as its market capitalization, show that the airline and other discounters must have overcome any residual safety concerns of the flying public and investors.

The June 1, 2004 issue of *Fortune* magazine carried an article entitled 'Why the Big Boys Won't Come Back' and subtitled 'For the nation's beleaguered airline industry, the tipping point is finally here: The discounters are winning'.

With the exception of Southwest and a few other low cost carriers, the entire airline industry has continued to bleed financially for the last several years.

Legacy carriers in bankruptcy include United and U.S. Airways, which announced plans in May 2005 to merge with formerly bankrupt America West. This combination will form the nation's fifth largest airline.

Legacy carriers Delta and Northwest both filed for Chapter 11 bankruptcy on September 14, 2005.

Commercial aviation financial crossroads

The U.S. airline industry lost $9.1 billion in 2004 (including Delta's $5.2 billion), according to government statistics compiled by Air Transport Association.

This is in addition to losses in each of the three prior years.

The industry outlook remains bleak with oil prices remaining consistently over $60 a barrel and a briefly spiking to over $70 as this book goes to press. Market prices for jet fuel correlate closely with the prices of crude oil.

The price of aviation fuel has continued to increase dramatically, along with the rise in crude oil prices, rising to $1.57 a gallon in June 2005, a 45% increase from a year before. It has moved much higher since then. For example, the effects of Hurricanes Katrina and Rita have kept the price during September 2005 above $1.80 per gallon, with spikes over $2.20.

Billionaire Warren Buffett, noted for his investment prowess, wrote off a several hundred million dollar investment in U.S. Airways. In an interview with Australian media in the fall of 2002, Buffett said, "...if a capitalist had been present at Kitty Hawk back in the early 1900's he should have shot Orville Wright. He would have saved his progeny money...You've got huge fixed costs, you've got strong labour unions and you've got commodity pricing. That is not a great recipe for success." He went on to say, "I have an 800 number now that I call if I get the urge to buy an airline stock. I call at two in the morning and I say, 'My name is Warren and I'm an aeroholic.' And then they talk me down."

Focus on Delta's Board and CEO

This book focuses on the internal story that was within the control of Delta's Board and top management, particularly its CEO. It examines particularly decisions that turned out wrong and suggests that the result was predictable – and therefore avoidable - in key situations.

Comprehensive, human story

The business story has been told in bits and pieces through articles in newspapers and magazines with incessant, almost daily, headlines.

Reading the headlines is like looking at pieces of a complex jigsaw puzzle and wondering how they might all fit together. This book gets behind the headlines to piece together the Delta story in a comprehensive way so the reader can see a more complete picture.

The story here is a human one as much as a business story. The human side of the CEOs, their values and their leadership style have arguably been the driving factor in affecting how Delta has responded to its business challenges throughout its history.

Delta people are an integral part of the people story. They have been phenomenal in their loyalty and dedication to the customer and the company in spite of obstacles thrown in their path by external factors and decisions made by the Board and CEOs. This loyalty and passion for the company is amazingly still alive, although seriously wounded, in spite of the financial and professional harm that Delta leaders have inflicted on thousands of Delta employees and retirees.

Delta people continue to make an extraordinary effort to overcome the financial and human mess left by the prior CEO and a Board that allowed it to happen.

It was sad to watch – and sadder still for employees and retirees - such effort still result in bankruptcy.

Introduction

The author and the book

The reader of any book, to judge its relevance and validity, has the right to know the credentials of the writer as well as the sources and methods of obtaining the information on which it is based.

Author's credentials to write this book

Extensive business and management consulting experience - For over 23 years, he has run his own firm as a consultant to senior management. He serves as a business strategist, sounding board, leadership expert and the voice of employees and customers for both *Fortune* 500 and entrepreneurial firms. Previously he was a marketing professional for 14 years on Madison Avenue and in Atlanta serving national accounts like Procter & Gamble. During his career, he has observed and helped develop many leaders in organizations of all sizes and geographic scopes.

Membership in the extended "Delta family" -

- Atlanta resident for 34 years

- Spouse was a Delta manager for over 26 years prior to accepting an offer from another firm (assuming Delta's survival and the survival of its pension plan, she will be eligible for a pension upon reaching retirement age). She was *not* an interviewee for this book.

- Father-in-law (deceased) was regional administrator for FAA and had high regard for Delta's safety commitment and integrity

- Extensive social interaction, including visiting in their homes and playing golf together, with Delta employees and senior executives
- Has met the 3 most recent Delta CEOs out of 7 total; a former neighbor of a 4th
- Knows 6 of the current top officers and 2 Board members
- Knows many current Delta employees
- Knows many former Delta employees and executives
- Reading company employee publications and other employee communications for many years; studying these further as part of research for the book
- Flying Delta many times domestically and internationally, including Canada, Mexico, Bermuda, Grand Cayman, St. Lucia, Paris and London
- Member of the Delta Employees Credit Union
- Small stockholder

How the book was researched

Interviews and conversations with 59 people – These ranged from several brief conversations to primarily in-depth confidential interviews, many lasting two hours or more. There were some multiple interviews with the same person. All are members of the

Introduction

"Delta family" in some way, including high mileage Medallion customers of many years:

- Delta executives – current and former
- Delta front-line employees – current and former
- CEOs of other companies
- Senior Executives / Professionals of other companies
- Executive Search Professionals
- Friends / acquaintances of Delta people

I asked interviewees the following questions:

- What has been your personal experience with Delta?
- What made Delta successful?
- When did you notice this changing?
- How did Delta get in the shape it is now?
- What do you see for Delta's future?

Please note that Mr. Allen's separation agreement, and probably Mr. Mullin's as well, included a 'mutual non-disparagement' clause (meaning that neither side could say anything but good about the other). Because of this clause, formal interviews with any of Delta's current officers would have been a wasted effort.

An interviewee told me that a similar clause is also in the termination agreements of the senior executives who departed after Mullin. This increased the challenge of getting accurate and in-depth information, but did not prevent it.

I was grateful to find how willing people were to be interviewed; only three of those I asked declined, one due to their overwhelming schedule and two who felt they had nothing to contribute.

Many suggested others to interview and I contacted these people. I could have interviewed at least 25 more people, but decided to cut off at 59. I stopped there once the picture of what happened at Delta became clear, based on a consistency of recollections and perceptions on major points among the interviewees.

My commitment to confidentiality led to an openness from interviewees. I was glad to find that there were very few instances where an interviewee appeared to "have an axe to grind". The "Delta family" has a refreshing passion about their company. Interviewees demonstrated this passion in their obvious desire to talk about the company and the generosity with their time. Many seemed as if they had been waiting for someone who cared about Delta to listen to their feelings and thoughts about the company.

The result was both broad and often very specific knowledge and insights into Delta, supporting my intent to be thorough, accurate and fair in this portrayal.

Review of periodical articles – Dozens of periodical articles from numerous newspapers and magazines over a period of 25 years were reviewed.

Review of relevant web sites – I reviewed several dozen web sites, including Delta's, competitive airlines, news media, unions and blogs.

Introduction

Review of relevant business cases from major universities

Review and analysis of Delta's financial and operating data

Review of Delta annual reports since the inception of the company in 1929

U.S. Department of Transportation airline operating and customer satisfaction statistics

Annual reports of competitive airlines

Read all previous books on Delta that I could find – These included:

- 1979 – "Delta: The History of an Airline" by Lewis and Newton published around Delta's 50th anniversary

- 1988 – "Delta Air Lines: Debunking The Myth" written by Davis. A critical review of Delta by a former executive

- 1990 – "Delta: The Illustrated History of a Major U.S. Airline and the People Who Made It." Delta history as told by extensive detail on the planes acquired and the fleet with executives interspersed. Commissioned by Ron Allen

- 1998 – "Delta Air Lines" written by Jones. An abbreviated history with extensive aircraft photos commissioned after the arrival of Leo Mullin in 1997

- 2003 – "Delta Air Lines: 75 years Of Airline Excellence" also by Jones. Written to commemorate Delta's 75th anniversary; commissioned by Leo Mullin

Review of information from Delta Air Transport Heritage Museum – This includes:

- Annual reports
- Company employee publications
- Videotapes
- Vintage aircraft.

I gratefully acknowledge the assistance provided by the museum. (A portion of the proceeds, after expenses, from sale of this book will be donated to the museum.)

Overview

This extensive research says clearly that the greatest impact on Delta's history has come from:

- The management style and leadership ability of the CEO
- The level of engagement of the Board of Directors
- Loyal, dedicated employees
- External events beyond Delta's direct control

The first two factors – CEO and the Board – directly and indirectly have affected the company's ability to deal effectively with the fourth factor – external events.

Delta employees have insisted on running a fine airline even when the first two factors were unfavorable

Hindsight is always 20/20; however, many interviewees share my belief that **key external factors were predictable and, with proper management**

leadership, their negative effect on Delta could have been minimized and perhaps avoided.

For example, an even cursory examination of the history of commercial aviation demonstrates a certain predictability about running an airline. Therefore, an airline's Board and CEO must consider these predictable factors in making every major decision:

- It requires high capital investment
- This capital investment is recurring, driven by new technology, new aircraft and the need to remain competitive
- Employee costs are the second major component
- Employees deliver the service to the customer so employee morale and commitment is essential to provide good service
- Leadership, or lack of it, at the top (Board and CEO) can dramatically affect the relationship with employees
- Wars come and go but at some point there will be another war
- The economy is cyclical with boom times and recessions
- World events can affect availability and costs of crude oil, so aviation fuel costs can vary widely

Because of the above factors, managing costs tightly is essential at all times in order to achieve sustained profitability. Cost management is important to help create financial integrity and be in control of an airline's destiny, as Delta's CEOs were from 1929 until

1987. This control provides the cushion to weather unfavorable external events.

Since it is predictable that unfavorable external events *will* reoccur (and the only unknown is *when*) if an airline's management cites such events as the reason their airline is in serious trouble that is *prima facie* evidence of a Board and management mistake or failure.

Because of the high probability an external event will reoccur, there must be a well-conceived contingency plan in place to deal with such an event long before it surfaces. When the event does occur, it becomes a simple matter for the CEO and management to switch immediately to 'Plan B', without panic or the need to develop a contingency plan under duress.

While taking an occasional 'hit' from an external event is a normal part of doing business, saying an external event seriously, and perhaps permanently, damaged an airline is not a reason. It is an excuse from ineffective leaders.

Delta's six 9/11's

I submit that Delta has experienced *six 9/11's*:

1966 – Founder C.E. Woolman died

1978 – Airlines deregulated

1987 – Ron Allen elected CEO

1997 – Leo Mullin elected CEO

2001 – Terrorists attack on U.S. soil

2005 – Bankruptcy filing on 9/14/05

By 9/11, I mean a potentially catastrophic event.

How the company – particularly the Board and the CEO – dealt with each of these events has greatly influenced the results and contributed to the situation in which the company finds itself today.

Two of Delta's 9/11s were in fact on that date – Mr. Woolman's death in 1966 and the World Trade Center attacks. The bankruptcy filing missed by 3 days.

By using 9/11 as the metaphor for other catastrophic events at Delta, by no means do I intend to minimize the pain or loss of those directly affected by the New York City attacks or the significance of those attacks.

My heart goes out to those who lost friends or loved ones in the terrorist attack on 9/11/2001. I have a friend that worked in one of the towers who, by the grace of God, was late for work that day and thus escaped with this life.

The role of the Board of Directors

Throughout the book, it will point out situations where Board leadership and involvement might have made a huge difference in bringing about a more favorable outcome.

Prior to the recent Enron and related scandals, there had been a power shift over several decades from Boards to management.

Sarbanes–Oxley has greatly increased management and Board responsibility and accountability in the financial arena.

I submit that Boards now must be held equally accountable for far more than the accuracy and validity of reported numbers.

Board's expanded role in CEO selection

That power shift resulted in a leader often having carte blanche to choose his successor, sometimes with harmful or even disastrous consequences. Delta is a prime example. I contend that these consequences are often predictable and avoidable with appropriate Board leadership and involvement.

Board's expanded role in management consulting

Another area where Board leadership and involvement has become increasingly essential is in the selection, direction, evaluation and termination of management consulting firms, particularly when they are engaged for projects affecting the whole company.

These firms can have a significant, negative long-term effect on a company. Many believe Delta is a good example.

The horse and the ditch

Leadership keeps the horse out of the ditch

The leadership perspective of this book is intended to address the issues cited by Xerox CEO Anne Mulcahy in the parable about her own challenges in turning around that company (*Fortune* issue of March 21, 2005):

- Get the horse out of the ditch.
- Find out how the horse got in the ditch.
- Make sure you do whatever it takes so the horse doesn't go into the ditch again.

Introduction

Delta now and Delta's future

Delta's horse is obviously "in the ditch", even to a casual observer.

Based on extensive research, the book provides insights and perspectives on how the Delta horse got there in the first place.

The company is working mightily right now to get the Delta horse "out of the ditch."

Survival is the top priority and then emerging from bankruptcy. Rebirth is down the road.

I hope this book will help leaders in any organization, including Delta, prevent the "horse" under their care from going into a ditch ever again.

I also make strategic and tactical suggestions intended to help Delta's CEO and Board get the "horse out of the ditch."

1 –Leadership

A search on the word 'leadership' in Google produces *176,000,000* results. This is an obvious indication of the high level of interest in the subject as well as the fact that many people think they have something worthwhile to say about it.

Leadership models

There are a lot of leadership models, each one usually purporting to be the Holy Grail of management. Of course, such models are often merely a consultant-branding attempt supported by the business media. Like most fads, another one replaces these; the cycle continues.

However, experience and common sense dictates there is no one model that is the end all / be all.

For example, many pundits consider the 'command and control' leadership model passé today. It is in vogue to support an 'employee empowerment' model or some other form of inclusiveness. There are often viable reasons for such an approach. However, I submit that most Marines in Iraq on patrol feel much safer if the leader uses the 'command and control' approach instead of trying to 'empower' them and their fellow soldiers in the midst of a firefight with the enemy.

The point here is that there are different leadership models – each with advantages and disadvantages. Every organization needs to evaluate itself and its needs to determine the leadership approach that works best.

In my consulting work, I have found it far more useful to the client to avoid the use of model terminology altogether and focus instead on a through understanding of the organization – its situation, goals, needs, people and the available leadership.

Principles of leadership

I have found there are useful leadership principles to consider when assessing an organization and helping them develop their own leadership model:

- Leadership is the key to an organization's sustained success.

- It is a relationship between the leader and its people built on:
  - Integrity
  - Trust
  - Mutual respect
  - Fairness
  - Competence
  - Courage

- A true leader is someone that people willingly follow. The opposite is dictatorship.

- The leader's heart is more important than brains. Brains are readily available; they can be hired and managed. Hearts are much harder to find.

- An effective leader 'walks the talk'. He/she understands that people watch what you do, not what you say.

- A leader is not someone who is a would-be king or queen.

- A leader of an organization humbly knows he/she has the potential to provide the foundation for the organization or to sew its seeds of destruction.

- Like a good physician, a leader approaches any issue or situation with a thorough, fact-based diagnosis before prescribing a cure. The leader also insists his/her people (and management consultants that are engaged) use the same kind of approach.

- A leader thoroughly analyzes all reasonable options before moving ahead. Like Procter & Gamble, a leader insists not only on a rationale for the preferred option but also a rationale on why other reasonable options are not recommended.

- A leader understands the Economics 101 "opportunity cost" concept. In evaluating options, the cost of *not doing* Option B is considered along with the cost of doing Option A.

- A leader, particularly a new one, follows the Hippocratic Oath of business: "Do no harm".

- A leader insists on an organizational antenna that is alert for potential emergencies to prevent their happening or to deal with them more effectively should they occur. With an operable antenna, many so called 'emergencies' are eminently predictable and thus manageable.

- A leader has a spirit of service – to customers, stockholders, employees and others affected by the organization.

- A leader appreciates the value of every job and every employee to the success of the organization – and continually demonstrates this appreciation. All are shown how they make a difference.

- A leader is transparent and predictable because his/her behavior is based on values known to everyone in the organization.

The history of Delta underscores the validity of the above principles of leadership.

A Board's top task is choosing the right leader and holding them accountable

I believe that the #1 fiduciary responsibility of a Board of Directors is to insure the survival of the organization.

To fulfill this responsibility requires great care and skill at selecting the right leader and then holding them appropriately accountable.

I have found through experience that *organizations are like people*. They each have their own unique personality, values and culture.

The first step of leader selection is determining whether the leader needs to be someone who can blend with the existing personality and mold it effectively or someone (like IBM's Board obviously decided before they brought in Lou Gerstner) who will dramatically alter the personality.

IBM, before Gerstner, had been built on the premise that its legions of managers should be hired and developed to become like interchangeable parts. The uniform of these faceless people was the blue suit and the white shirt.

Leadership

In the late 1960's, one of my apartment mates in New York City was an audit senior for Price Waterhouse, IBM's public accounting firm. As a member of the PW audit team, he traveled to IBM's Armonk headquarters on the first day of the audit. My friend made the mistake of wearing a blue shirt. As a result, the CFO of IBM called the IBM partner at PW to demand that my friend be sent home to change into a white shirt.

While this kind of thinking was part of IBM's culture and growth for decades, it became a liability. Their Board recognized that and brought in Gerstner to change it. Today, my IBM friends wear open collar shirts and the company is far more successful than it was before.

Delta is in the opposite situation. Its culture is still valid and meaningful. Their problem has been the lack of understanding of that culture's value and support of it from the CEO and the Delta Board.

At the highest levels of most major U.S. businesses today, unfortunately leader selection is done through a closed network of interlocking friendships and business affiliations. The question of the potential leader's ability to interface effectively with the organization's personality is never asked.

These interpersonal relationships often completely overshadow the most important relationship – the one between the leader and the organization.

As a result, the due diligence regarding a candidate becomes more what those in the network (in the South it is referred to as the "Good Ole Boys") tell each other about the individual rather a candid evaluation of the likelihood of success in the new leadership role.

There is often a focus on the individual's experience or accomplishments in a current position. However, unless the personality of the current team or organization is comparable to the prospective one, then "past performance is no guarantee of future results," just as it is not with mutual funds.

Regrettably, there are readily available tools, at a reasonable cost, to get a good bead on the inner nature of a prospective leader – whether internal or from outside the organization.

Then there are related tools to effectively determine the correlation between the nature of the person and what is needed for the position and the organization.

From experience, using these tools appropriately will greatly increase the accuracy of the person's probability of success as a leader *in a specific organization and a specific job.*

The importance of the Board making this determination in advance is to protect the organization – its stockholders, employees and customers – as well as the individual from a high risk of failure.

For example, I have used these tools to help a client select an executive to fill successfully what had been a high turnover, problem position. Equally important, I have used these tools to help clients eliminate from consideration prospective leaders who, on paper, appeared to be good choices but who had a demonstrably low probability of success.

Valuable information on a person such tools can provide are:

Overall behavior profile – typical behavior of the individual

Leadership

Leadership profile – likely behavior in a leadership role

Motivating factors – individual's needs, to insure the organization and position would meet them

Team approach – how he/she works in a team; particularly important to understand the fit within the dynamics of an existing team

Learning style – how the person learns in order to help guide them, particularly in the first few weeks of a new job

Selling style – how they sell their ideas or solutions to others

Coaching / development strategies – how best to approach the individual when behavior needs to be modified

Armed with the above information, the Board is in a far better position to make wise decisions about people for leadership roles.

If the individual is hired or promoted, the Board is also in a far better position to manage intelligently the leader for the organization's benefit as well as that of the leader.

Unfortunately, this modified 'try before you buy' approach is atypical. However, it works.

Given the high cost of leader failure and the increasing frequency of these failures at the CEO level, today's Boards must adopt a proactive approach to reduce their risk using available tools to do this.

Based on the research for this book, I believe that if an approach like the above had been followed by Delta's Board, Leo Mullin would have not been hired as

CEO; it is unlikely that Ron Allen would have been promoted to CEO either.

The point here is that the examples of Mullin's leadership failure and Allen's less than effective leadership arguably were predictable and, therefore, preventable.

Changing relationship between CEOs and Boards of Directors

Prior to Sarbanes – Oxley, Boards of Directors in the U.S. frequently became rubber stamps for management.

This phenomenon came about as the power in large organizations increasingly shifted over the years from shareholders, whose interests the Board is supposed to represent, to management, whose interests they now more often represent.

Implementation of strategies and tactics that were predictably destructive to the organization has been allowed because of Board ignorance or lethargy.

Recently, Boards have increasingly begun to step to the plate to hold CEOs accountable. This trend was fueled by the government coming down hard on improper, misleading or downright fraudulent financial reporting by corporations. Sarbanes-Oxley now requires the public company CEO, along with the CFO, to sign off on financial statements.

Government indictments have brought down once powerful CEOs like Bernie Ebbers of WorldCom and Ken Lay and Harvard MBA Jeffrey Skilling of Enron. Ebbers is on his way to prison. Lay's and Skilling's trials are forthcoming. Tyco CEO Dennis Kozlowksi and CFO Mark Schwartz recently were sentenced to 8 - 25 years in prison after their convictions for looting the company of hundreds of millions of dollars.

The law and public pressure now demands the Board of a publicly held corporation proactively take steps to prevent such corporate thievery in the future.

The decline of 'rock star' CEOs

As part of their increased engagement and oversight, Boards in the first 6 months of 2005:

- Terminated well known 'rock star' CEO's Carly Fiorina from Hewlett Packard (for non-performance when HP stock lost value after her Compaq merger)

- Franklin D. Raines from Freddie Mac (fear of scandal from increased government scrutiny).

- Harry C. Stonecipher, Boeing CEO, was forced by his Board to resign (extramarital relationship, which he refused to end, with an employee).

- Wal-Mart (on whose Board former Delta CFO Michele Burns now sits) Board member, Thomas C. Coughlin, formerly the #2 executive in the company resigned from the Board after an internal probe showed financial improprieties of as much as $500,000.

- Mike Eisner, long-time Disney CEO, is being forced out early by his Board.

- Maurice R. Greenberg, at the helm of insurance giant A.I.G. for decades, was ousted by his Board.

- Even Kofi Annan, Secretary General of the United Nations, is under scrutiny. He is in the midst of allegations regarding major financial improprieties of his subordinates and his son in the Oil For Food Program scandal. There are allegations that Annan himself lined his personal pockets as well.

Boardroom culture changes to skepticism

In a Wall Street Journal article dated March 15, 2005 Arthur Levitt, Jr., former head of the Securities and Exchange Commission said, "The fraternal culture that characterized America's Boards is undergoing a dramatic change to a culture of skepticism." He continued, "The humility and embarrassment of the past few years, combined with regulation, have changed the culture of boardrooms."

Personal financial liability of Board members fuels need to manage CEO

Contributing to the 'culture of skepticism' is the real financial liability and exposure of individual Board members, Directors and Officers Liability Insurance notwithstanding.

Recent landmark settlements have included the directors of WorldCom paying $18 million *out of their own pockets* and directors of Enron paying $13 million *out of their own pockets*.

Even directors of a financial institution now need to be on heightened alert about the customers of their institution. In March 2005 14 banks accepted a $6 billion out of court settlement to compensate WorldCom investors, $5 billion to bondholders and $1 billion to stockholders. This settlement cost Citigroup $2.58 billion and J.P. Morgan Chase $2 billion.

The WorldCom class action settlement was reportedly by far the largest recovery in history. The plaintiffs contended that the banks should have known that WorldCom's financial statements were fraudulent and learned this as part of the process of underwriting the company's bonds.

A Florida state court jury in May, 2005 awarded financier Ronald Perelman $604.3 million in compensatory damages and $850 million in punitive damages after finding well-known investment banking firm Morgan Stanley guilty of fraud. Perelman sold Coleman, his camping-gear company, to Morgan Stanley client, Sunbeam, in 1998.

Public accounting firms no longer icons

This pressure, and the widespread publicity surrounding it, was also a major factor in the demise of Arthur Andersen, once the largest public accounting firm in the world. The firm was convicted for obstruction of justice because their Houston office allegedly shredded related documents during the government investigation of Enron. Recently the U.S. Supreme Court overturned the conviction on the grounds the jury instructions were too broad. A decision on a retrial is pending.

Multi-million lawsuits with big CPA firms as defendants are now commonplace.

The website, www.accountingmalpractice.com, chronicles the wrongdoing in a profession that once was the icon for financial integrity.

This is a worldwide phenomenon. Recently in Norway, KPMG reached an out-of-court settlement to pay eight banks $53.6 million in damages because of the firm's role in a large Norwegian bankruptcy.

News media no longer get a free pass

Even the news media has lost its exemption from scrutiny.

CBS news anchor Dan Rather lost his credibility along with ratings after broadcasting a fake memo regarding the President's military service. Rather eventually expressed "regret" at the major journalistic error after "sticking with the story" long after most viewers had determined Rather's source was a fake. CBS allowed him to stick around for a few months before retiring him from his anchor position.

Howell Raines, Executive Editor of the venerable New York Times, resigned following the revelation of repeatedly fabricated stories by protégé Jayson Blair.

The Times recently has again come under scrutiny for their misleading story about Geraldo Rivera.

Mandatory for Boards to step to the plate

This entire chapter graphically underscores the fact it is no longer optional for a Board to exercise proactively its fiduciary responsibility to insure a corporation's survival and to pick the right CEO and oversee them.

2 – Culture

"The notion that capitalism is America's true religion is one of those profundities repeated so often that it ceases to be profound. It also misses the mark. Companies are not churches. But the strongest of them, like the strongest churches, are more than stone edifice and empty ritual. They're communities of true believers." – Jerry Useem, *Fortune*, September 19, 2005

The meaning of culture in this book is focused on organizations.

Culture is the collection of commonly held paradigms – perspectives based on values and attitudes - that determine acceptable behavior traits in an organization.

Culture creates the environment in which all decisions are made, all actions are judged and all results measured.

While some organizations have a culture similar to others, no two are exactly alike. Often the differences are far greater than the similarities.

Culture produces and defines the unique personality of an organization – the behavioral traits that are visible to employees, customers and others.

Culture and acquisitions

These differences are what make post-merger acquisitions so difficult.

For example, the cultural differences between Silicon Valley legend HP and PC giant Compaq created huge obstacles to that merger. The difficulty in overcoming those obstacles surely contributed to the lackluster performance of the combined company and the departure of CEO Carly Fiorina.

One of my clients, the U.S. subsidiary of a global company, acquired another company in a related business. The headquarters of the two companies were 700 miles apart, which produced geographic cultural differences initially. The acquired company also differed because it was a closely held family business. Most important, the customer contact employees of the acquiring company were more highly skilled and trained than those of the one acquired. The latter difference required major management effort, with outside assistance from my firm, over a period of 18 months to resolve effectively.

How culture develops

The foundation of culture is **values**. The CEO is instrumental in defining and reinforcing an organization's values. Therefore, hiring or promoting a CEO with the desired values is key to the culture of the organization. Values are the basic beliefs of a person or organization

Values produce **attitudes**, the ways in which a person views the world, other people, the organization, and themselves.

Widely held **attitudes** then become the **culture** of an organization or group.

Culture then creates **behavior traits (personality)** of the organization, team or group.

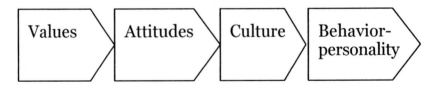

Values → Attitudes → Culture → Behavior-personality

Culture and the leader

A leader has a huge impact on an organization's culture and, therefore, its behavior.

A strong leader's imprint can last long after they are gone. Delta Air Lines, Inc. is an excellent case history. The flame lit by Mr. C.E. Woolman prior to his death in 1966 has fueled Delta ever since. It continues to flicker even in the midst of the current devastated situation of the company.

Mr. Woolman's strongly held values manifested themselves in important attitudes. Delta executives and employees adopted these values and attitudes. Those unwilling to adopt them were either never hired or eased out the door once the disconnect became apparent.

For example, fairness was one of Mr. Woolman's key values. His attitude was that employees needed to be treated fairly. This attitude forged a culture where management compensation and perquisites were limited by what the other employees received. In addition, customers were the priority over executives or other employees.

Had anyone proposed to Woolman a pension trust scheme to provide greater protection for executive pensions than that offered employees (like the one Leo Mullin and Delta's Board approved in 2002) quite probably they would have been fired on the spot and escorted off the premises.

Woolman, in anticipation of his retirement or death, once hired a CEO-in-waiting. This individual never set foot on Delta property as an employee. He had the audacity to insist that a Delta plane in New York

City be held for his arrival because he was late getting to the airport.

Dr. William Mayo and his two physician sons started world famous Mayo Clinic in rural Minnesota. Over 100 years ago, they developed a new vision of medicine as a "cooperative science" with different experts "uniting for the good of the patient.

I have been a patient of Mayo Clinic for over 10 years and can attest that every employee and professional continues to implement this vision every day.

Like Mr. Woolman, the values and attitudes of the Mayo father and sons have been transferred to generations of others on their team.

Mr. Woolman developed a culture of 'the customer comes first'. The Mayo family developed a culture of 'the patient comes first'.

In both cases, that organization's culture attracted like-minded people who passed it on to newcomers and then reinforced it to make sure it stuck.

Recently, I was undergoing an echocardiogram at Mayo Clinic. I noticed that the technician, although quite young and new to the clinic, appeared very professional and very serious about her work. When asked what prompted her to apply for her position, she said simply, "I wanted to be with a medical institution where the patient is the focus and this is it."

That young woman is a spiritual heir to the three long dead founders.

Anyone doubting the significance of the CEO and the culture to the viability and future of an organization need only recall this story.

Fortunately for the Mayo Clinic, its leaders through the years have been selected to embrace and continue the culture. This is in direct contrast to Delta in recent years, as this book documents.

Culture and the role of the Board

If one agrees with the premise that the #1 priority of a Board of Directors is the survival of the organization, then the obvious corollary is the Board's fiduciary responsibility for the culture.

A key part of this fiduciary responsibility is selecting a CEO who will embrace and reinforce a valuable culture like that initiated by Mr. Woolman or the Mayo Clinic founders. Conversely, it entails leaving no stone unturned to insure that the organization is spared from the harm and potential destruction of a CEO who is unwilling to take up the cause.

Another crucial element of a Board's fiduciary responsibility is to prevent outside business partners from damaging the culture. This is true particularly of management consulting firms.

While a consulting firm's work in an individual business unit has the potential for cultural harm, the Board's appropriate focus is on enterprise-wide consulting projects and ongoing retainer relationships. The latter are much more likely to harm the entire organization.

The Board also needs to focus on long-term, enterprise-wide projects that employees alone plan and implement, since these carry a risk of organizational harm as well.

For the above reasons, I recommend Boards establish a **Strategic Culture Committee**.

This committee has multiple responsibilities:

- Determine the organization's historical and existing values, attitudes, culture and personality

- Decide which are essential to preserve, which are desirable but not essential and which are detrimental

- Present findings and recommendations to the full Board for review and approval

- Proactively implement the Board approved plan which will include at least the following:

    - In general exercise oversight of the organization's strategy and culture

    - Review and report to the full Board on all:

        - Strategic plans and strategic initiatives proposed by management

        - Proposed enterprise wide projects

        - Proposed long-term projects or ongoing retainer contracts with management consultants

- Exercise the same degree of involvement and oversight for employee policies and compensation (comparable to existing Personnel and Compensation Committees which generally focus on senior management)

- Vigorously oppose any proposals, actions or prospective CEO's that are likely to harm the culture or strategically damage the organization

This Committee will be the Board's conscience.

3 – Birth – Teenage Years

"The final test of a leader is that he leaves behind him in other men the conviction and the will to carry on." – Author unknown

By the above measure, C.E. Woolman was an outstanding leader

How Delta started

Mr. Woolman co-founded Delta in 1925 as an aerial crop dusting operation. The company was a pioneer in efficiently spreading the insecticide calcium arsenate over cotton fields in the South to control the deadly boll weevil.

Out of deference to Mr. Woolman, Delta continued to offer crop dusting service, although it became a minor part of the company, until 1966, the year in which the founder died.

Delta became an airline in 1929 when Woolman and his business associates decided to offer passenger service from Dallas to Birmingham via several points en route. (Sadly, one of the recent cost cutting moves was to shut down Delta's base in Dallas where the company initiated airline operations 76 years ago.)

The long shadow of one man

Rarely has one man's shadow so infused a business in this country as Mr. Woolman's has infused Delta throughout its entire history.

Although he died 39 years ago, a large, but declining number of Delta people even today share and practice the foundational values Mr. Woolman laid.

Lessons in Leadership

Delta retirees fondly recall the man, the values and the decades when everyone in the company embraced them. Those interviewed retain a passion for the company and everything for which it stood while they were working there. They wistfully recall the better times when the behavior of Delta leaders invariably demonstrated those values. There is a longing to help restore them.

Unfortunately, as this book documents, the Delta Board selected and supported top executives from outside the company who not only did not share these values but also demonstrated a belief they are anachronisms. The results from those leaders are predictably disastrous. Their 180° departure from what made Delta successful was probably the key factor leading to the bankruptcy.

Interviewees pointed out the hypocrisy of these leaders playing to the crowd of true believers in the Delta culture by trumpeting the words of Mr. Woolman in speeches, annual reports and employee communications. Over time, it became obvious these leaders honored his words only in the breach.

Interviewees also identified a current Delta senior leader and long-term employee who is 'talking the talk' because it is the politically correct thing to do; yet their walk is no different from the now departed harmful outsiders and equally detrimental. Yet this individual has successfully positioned themselves as the one most knowledgeable about Delta's tradition and culture.

True leadership

Mr. Woolman was a true leader. He understood intuitively and practiced what some self-proclaimed management gurus try to espouse today as if they discovered something brand new.

A business has to make a profit, but the foundation of a company are its people and the customers those people serve. This is particularly true in a service business like an airline.

When the CEO sets the pace for all the senior leaders to appreciate the employees, treat them fairly and give them the tools needed to serve the customer the organization will prosper.

Stated simply, **"When the employees are happy, the customers will be happy."**

That approach produced Delta's employee, customer and financial success for almost 7 decades.

Leadership vacuum

The new leader in 1997, Leo Mullin, took a different approach. He demonstrated values and attitudes that resulted in what employees and most observers, then and now, believe was unfair treatment of employees. A complicit Board permitted and supported him.

That unfair treatment, combined with questionable major financial decisions, started Delta on a downward spiral that first became clearly visible in early 2001. The speed of that spiral has increased and continues downward throughout fall 2005.

Woolman's simple business formula

Mr. Woolman's formula was simple but quite sophisticated.

He was unwavering in living and espousing these values and beliefs, which he imparted to every member of the "Delta family". These values and beliefs produced the Delta culture and personality.

The formula below has stood the test of time well.

Integrity

Mr. Woolman's word was his bond. He said what he meant and meant what he said. His integrity was known throughout the industry and was a major asset for Delta.

As one retired pilot said, "Mr. Woolman and Donald Douglas [patriarch of Douglas aircraft, Delta's exclusive supplier for decades] would sit around a table with a fifth of bourbon and then do a deal [for many planes and millions of dollars] on a handshake."

Customer service

Mr. Woolman constantly reminded employees "we must always put ourselves on the other side of the counter."

His daughter, Barbara Woolman Preston, in a videotaped 1997 interview, said her father would often bring a passenger home for lunch or dinner if a Delta flight were delayed. She also reported how, as a little girl, she would occasionally wake up on a couch. Her father would have brought home a stranded passenger to spend the night and then given them her bed.

Teamwork

Although Mr. Woolman oversaw the company with a firm hand, I found no indication that he ever thought he could do it alone.

He had great ego strength and the courage of his convictions, but it never seemed to spill over into arrogance or executive elitism. A quote from him in the 1991 annual report is corroboration:

"No one person is an airline. An airline is a team."

Family

Much has been written through the years about the "Delta family". In that same 1991 annual report, the above quote continues:

"It [an airline] must be friendly, courteous, cooperative, efficient, and bound as closely as a devoted family."

A fundamental part of the family was treating each other fairly and respectfully. "Delta family" members quickly learned to count on each other. They also learned that management compensation was reasonable.

They learned that when management asked employees to endure temporary financial pain, due to business conditions, management would share equally in that pain.

Delta followed a 'promote from within' policy. This produced intense loyalty along with sometimes insular thinking.

A key management strategy for decades was to pay Delta people better than any other airline. This strategy has been a key reason most Delta employees are non-unionized. The pilots unionized almost from the beginning and have continued to be unionized.

Safety

From the beginning, this has been a top priority.

Heart

"As a man thinketh in his heart, so is he." - Proverbs 23:7

"...for of the abundance of the heart, his mouth speaketh." – Luke 6:45

Service - and leadership - must start with the heart to be genuine and lasting.

In a short film from the early 1960's, apparently prepared to show at a system-wide station managers meeting, Mr. Woolman said:

"Delta has enjoyed a steady growth through the years [but] one thing is unchanged:

The concept of customer service expressed in our slogan

SERVICE AND HOSPITALITY FROM THE HEART.

We have always tried to put ourselves on the other side of the counter and treat our passengers as we would like to be treated.

We believe that an airline has a responsibility to the public over and above the price of a ticket.

We try to live up to that responsibility."

Stewardship

Delta started its airline business in 1929, the year the Great Depression began. To survive that experience leading a new company in a new industry, Mr. Woolman watched every nickel earned and spent by Delta. He also understood revenue generation, constantly reminding his city agents to "get me one more passenger" on each flight.

He would pick up paper clips and rubber bands off the floor or a desk to recycle them. An interviewee who worked around Mr. Woolman said he felt compelled, because of the Woolman example, to reuse paper clips and rubber bands and to conserve costs in every way.

If a headquarters employee needed office supplies, they could only get them by making a request at the storeroom window. The clerk gave out only one legal pad; if they requested more, the clerk told the employee to return when they had used that one up.

Woolman focused employee frugality on internal costs while making sure to spend the necessary money on passenger comforts to remain competitive.

While this frugality may seem a bit silly to some today, it was instrumental in putting and keeping Delta on the road to a consecutive string of profitable years unprecedented in the airline industry.

Woolman also clearly understood the importance of putting aside money during the good years to prepare for the inevitable lean years in the airline business. Throughout its history, commercial aviation has been cyclical. Extremes in the total economy, fuel prices and wars are examples of factors that consistently have a direct impact on an airline and the industry.

He also understood the need for fiscal conservatism to be in a position to make the capital investments necessary to utilize new aircraft and technology.

Cost-conscious behavior manifested itself throughout Delta from 1929 until 1987 when it began to erode under new CEO Ron Allen. After Leo Mullin became CEO in 1997, Delta became a spendthrift; this behavior was instrumental in bringing Delta to its financial knees and now bankruptcy.

Mr. Woolman's prudence in avoiding waste reminds me of an experience when I was a volunteer responsible for the marketing communications for one of Atlanta's annual United Way campaigns. Although my time and that of others in my firm was provided pro bono, some out of pocket expenses were necessary for United Way to pay. It became necessary to approach the campaign leadership for a several thousand dollar increase in the budget to help achieve a multi-million campaign goal. The request was granted.

Mr. Ed Rast, then CEO of Southern Bell and a man from the same mold as Mr. Woolman, put his arm around my shoulder as I left the meeting and said, "Son, don't spend all that money if you don't have to." I am frugal, particularly with money of others. However, Mr. Rast successfully prompted my extra effort to figure out ways to get the job done and still not use up all the additional appropriation.

Cost control

Mr. Woolman continually watched the expenses of the company and was never embarrassed to ask employees, and sometimes their families, to help him. For example, he asked the wife of Nip Hill, a Delta employee since 1935, to launder, press and return the seat cloths. After months of providing this free service to Delta, Mrs. Hill balked. Mr. Woolman resolved the situation by setting up Mrs. Hill in a commercial laundry business with Delta as her first customer.

Financial sense

An important behind-the-scenes figure in Delta's financial integrity and profitability was Bob Oppenlander. He joined the company in 1958 as controller and in 1964 became Chief Financial Officer, a position he held for 23 years until his retirement.

Oppenlander, a brilliant man, combined financial acumen with sound business judgment. In recognition of his value to the company, stockholders elected him to the Board of Directors.

Oppenlander was instrumental in Delta moving from an all piston engine fleet to an all jet fleet during the 1960's. In his succinct but poignant style, he said jets "fly twice as far, twice as fast", as the Lewis book reports. The all jet fleet changed Delta's cost structure by enabling a dramatic reduction in fuel cost and, as a result, a lower cost per available seat mile.

Until 1987, Delta's Chief Financial Officer occupied an important seat at the table when all major strategic and financial decisions were being made. This makes sense in a capital intensive, competitive industry like the airline industry, where capital decisions and cost decisions can make or break the company.

In stark contrast to his predecessors, Ron Allen chose to exclude his Chief Financial Officer, Tom Roeck, from the 4 person Executive Council that ran Delta. This decision is hard to comprehend since Delta made major financial decisions and strategic decisions with long-term financial implications during Allen's tenure.

Among those decisions was the purchase of $450 million of assets from Pan Am.

Woolman's management style

Mr. Woolman's management style was based on pragmatism and common sense, combined with his thorough understanding of the airline business and Delta.

Woolman developed and practiced his management approaches long before today's self-appointed management "gurus", publicized by the business media, began trying to brand them as their own.

Servant leadership

He and the executive team were there to serve the Delta people to enable them to serve the customer successfully. Mr. Woolman understood this concept decades before it became a popular term and concept in business literature.

His humility and recognition of his servant role comes through in his words and reports of his actions even today.

Accessibility

Every employee was permitted and encouraged to contact any supervisor or executive at any level, including Mr. Woolman.

As Delta grew in size, geography and employees, in-person accessibility of management became more difficult but it continued.

As in-person opportunities declined, written communications increased.

Mr. Woolman consistently received and responded to letters from many Delta people, including those at the front line.

Treating employees as valued associates and with dignity and respect

It appears there was a policy to respond to all written communications from employees to management.

Mr. Woolman set the tone for these responses. No matter how irrelevant or unrealistic a suggestion might be, he patiently and graciously responded. Gratitude for writing accompanied each response.

One story has been told of a letter to Mr. Woolman from a front-line employee – in this case a flight attendant – with an impractical suggestion. His fatherly letter in response ended with a 'thank you' for taking the time to write and an invitation to write again.

Mr. Woolman's only known hobby was growing orchids, which he gave occasionally as a gesture of thanks to members of the "Delta family." These were highly prized.

Long-time Delta customers will recall the 'Flying Colonel' designation that the company awarded to special male customers and friends. Less well known is the 'Flying Orchid' designation (recalling Mr. Woolman's orchid gifts) which was given to special female customers and friends.

Management by walking around

Mr. Woolman proactively stayed in constant contact with the front line employees through personal visits to where they worked.

Like any good leader, he used these visits for multiple purposes including:

- Listening to employee concerns
- Demonstrating an appreciation of the work being done and its value to Delta
- Communicating and reinforcing management initiatives while seeking support for them
- Seeking first hand knowledge of inefficiencies, waste and ways to improve effectiveness
- Insuring the filtered information given him as CEO squares with the facts
- Exercising the experience that employees respect what they know the leader will inspect

More important than all the above purposes was his never ceasing effort to share his values, teach them to all employees and build a "Delta family."

Mr. Woolman made it a practice to learn the names and get to know hundreds of Delta employees. As an aid, he had his secretary prepare a "briefing book" before visiting any business unit or station. The book, which he reviewed while in transit, contained the name and photograph of each person Mr. Woolman was likely to see along with important business and personal information about him or her.

This "high touch" approach endeared him to Delta employees, produced high morale and helped generate a depth of loyalty about which most CEO's today only dream.

Long before the pop psychologists figured out that a person's name is one of the most important sounds in the world, Mr. Woolman's heart and head led him to recognize that essential reality about people.

Humility

Throughout all the extensive research in writing this book, I found no evidence of any arrogance or condescension in anything written about Mr. Woolman or in any of his written or spoken remarks.

On the contrary, he was a man of humility who demonstrated a gratitude and appreciation to have the opportunity to serve as the head of the "Delta family" he helped create and which he dearly loved.

He not only deferred to employees but also to passengers. When he decided to fly to visit a station, it was often spontaneous based on instinct.

Woolman would walk to the gate and find a vantage point where he could see but that was far enough away that is was not obvious to gate agents he was watching. Only when satisfied that all passengers had been accommodated would he approach the agent and request a seat. This directly contrasts with incidents under Mullin when, for example, an executive bumped passengers to accommodate their kids in first class.

Hands on management

Although he ran a sizable and growing company, Mr. Woolman did most of his own filing, according to an interviewee who worked directly with him.

He particularly handled his own filing on applications for new routes for Delta.

The primary avenue to airline growth, until deregulation in 1978, was by receiving authorization from the Federal government for a new route.

The process for securing these routes was long, time consuming, extremely detailed and constantly evolving.

Dozens of documents and statistics were required to support an airline's application in a route case. Adding to the paperwork complexity was the necessity to prepare all needed information by hand, since computers were not available then.

In addition, airlines competing for a potential route solicited the support of customers; the leaders in cities affected by route; and elected officials at all levels.

When the people complexity was added to the paperwork complexity and the financial and strategic importance to Delta of each route case is considered, it becomes easy to understand why the boss kept control of the process every step of the way.

An interviewee who worked directly with Mr. Woolman on rate cases recall how he would allow them to remove a document from one of the stacks behind his desk. However, he insisted on refiling the document himself because he had an exact place for each one.

This contrasts with the laissez faire style of management of Leo Mullin. The results of each leader speak for themselves.

Private Employee Assistance Program

Long before today's companies created formal programs to assist employees with personal, emotional or job related concerns, Mr. Woolman quietly set up and single-handedly ran such a program.

He kept the records for this program in a locked closet in his office. A reliable eyewitness related to me the incredible experience of sorting through these records following Mr. Woolman's death.

The closet contained dozens of handwritten letters from employees requesting help with a variety of problems.

Mr. Woolman personally responded to every one of these requests.

There was a separate stack for each individual employee. A stack contained all correspondence from the employee to Mr. Woolman and a copy of his response to them.

Warm heart and tough love

Mr. Woolman's warm heart clearly showed through these years of correspondence.

Most often, the requests were for money for things like unexpected medical bills or living costs.

If he thought the request had merit and the employee was loyal to Delta, he would grant the request. However, he would write something like, "You know that the company is not able to provide this money from its funds, so I am doing it personally."

He also made it clear the money was a loan, not a gift. In general, there was no due date or payment schedule. Instead, he said simply "pay this back a little at a time when you can."

Woolman kept meticulous records of these loans. On top of each employee's separate stack of correspondence was an envelope. On the back of that envelope Mr. Woolman recorded the date and amount of every payment.

After an employee repaid a loan, Mr. Woolman would write to congratulate them and tell them how proud of them he felt.

He exhibited tough love by holding every loan recipient accountable. If one requested a subsequent loan without having made an effort to settle the last one, Mr. Woolman would decline the request and tell them he would only reconsider if they demonstrated better stewardship of their money in the future.

Through all the correspondence, whether or not he granted a request, Mr. Woolman conveyed his concern and love for the individual employee and their family, often referring to members by name.

Mr. Woolman reported his repayment rate was over 75%.

The "Delta family" was and is a reality

Skeptics have questioned whether the "Delta family" spirit ever existed and, if it did, whether it was a strength or a weakness of Delta. My research and my personal experience tell me there is no question it has been a major strength for decades. Long after his death, and to some smaller degree today, the family spirit has continued.

As this book is intended to demonstrate, while Delta has faced significant external obstacles that have made it difficult, the main problem for the "Delta family" for a 17-year period was the company's top leader, and this problem was initiated, permitted or supported by the Board of Directors.

Delta experiences its first 9/11

Delta is the only airline to have experienced six 9/11's.

The first was 9/11/1966 when Mr. Woolman passed away after 37 years as the company's 'general manager', the term he preferred for his role.

His grave sits on a lovely knoll, overlooking a lake and gazebo, in a suburban Atlanta cemetery, along with those of his wife, two daughters and a son-in-law. All the graves have only a simple, but classic ground marker with a name, date of birth and date of death. This seems very much in keeping with the values he held during his life.

On the day Mr. Woolman died Delta employees everywhere stood and openly cried in a fitting emotional response to the beloved patriarch and leader of their family.

4 – Early Adult– Maturity

The Delta story unfolding after Mr. Woolman's death is basically one of the successes the company enjoyed when his leadership lessons were observed and the harm to the company when they were ignored.

"The genius of a good leader is to leave behind him a situation which common sense, without the grace of genius, can deal with successfully." – Walter Lippman

As the performance of the Delta during the tenure of the three CEO's in this 21-year chapter in Delta's life demonstrates, Mr. Woolman had that genius.

Beyond the period up to this day, Woolman believers have displayed extraordinary effort to run an airline based on the principles he espoused and taught them.

Woolman-trained Delta employees carry on

From the moment of Mr. Woolman's death forward, the Delta people steeped in his values, beliefs, and attitudes have taken a leadership role in running the airline. They have admirably worked hard to fulfill this role, even through tough times. In later years, these tough times included top management with questionable qualifications and values.

A former long-time employee characterized his pre-1987 experience with Delta in this way. "In the early days it was an incredible place to work. There was a spirit of cooperation; loyalty; dedication to the company; dedication to the customer; support of the employees."

3 CEOs help Delta reach maturity

There was a succession of 3 Chief Executive Officers, all associates of Mr. Woolman, during the 21-year period from 1966 to 1987:

- Charles Dolson – 1966 – 1971
- W.T. Beebe – 1971 – 1978
- David Garrett – 1978 – 1987

Building on the foundation laid by Mr. Woolman, although none of these CEOs had his presence or leadership ability, individually and collectively they were part of building an increasingly successful company.

At the core of this success was the help of thousands of loyal, professional Delta employees.

In spite of all the usual growth pains of any expanding company and external factors like deregulation Delta employees kept alive the Woolman legacy – his values, beliefs, attitudes and the resulting culture.

Woolman influenced Dolson and Garrett

Dolson CEO from 1966- 1971

In 1965, a year before CEO Woolman's death, Dolson became President of Delta. Under Dolson, in 1970 Delta's passenger fleet became all jet. Upon Mr. Woolman's death, he became CEO.

Dolson joined Delta in 1934 as a pilot after American furloughed him. During World War II, he was head of the Pacific branch of the Naval Air Transport Service.

Early Adulthood - Maturity

Beebe CEO from 1971 - 1978

W.T. "Tom" Beebe joined Delta when it merged with Chicago & Southern (C&S) Airlines on May 1, 1953. Beebe had worked at United Aircraft before becoming Director of Personnel at C&S in 1946. A year after the merger Beebe became Vice President – Personnel at Delta. Later he became Senior Vice President – Administration.

Mr. Woolman reportedly embraced the former C&S executives as members of the "Delta family" This gave Beebe exposure to Mr. Woolman's values, beliefs and practices.

In 1970, Dolson moved to Chairman and Beebe became President. Upon Dolson's retirement a year later, Beebe was named Chairman and CEO.

At the same time Beebe was elevated, David C. "Dave" Garrett was made President. Garrett joined Delta in 1946 and became Senior Vice President - Operations in 1967.

Beebe was known as somewhat aloof. The Davis book paints quite an unflattering picture of the man.

I had one experience with Beebe. A friend in Dallas had shipped a valuable show animal to me in Atlanta for temporary safekeeping. I shipped the animal back to Dallas on Delta. When the animal did not arrive at its destination on the scheduled flight, a number of phone calls determined that it had mistakenly been sent to Detroit. A Delta employee had misread the airport code on the shipping tag (Dallas code is DFW and Detroit code is DTW). Although many non-stop flights from Detroit to Dallas were available on other airlines, Delta would only return the animal to Atlanta and then ship it to

Dallas. The net effect was a 10-12 hour trip on multiple flights instead of a direct short flight.

A letter to Mr. Beebe protesting the refusal to put the animal on a direct flight from Detroit to Dallas produced a flabbergasting response. These were not the exact words, but the gist of the letter was "Our information shows that Delta harms fewer animals than other airlines and has fewer pet deaths." Although it is unlikely that Mr. Beebe wrote the letter or even saw it, it did come out under his name and signature so the responsibility remained with him.

In spite of any shortcomings of Beebe, a retired pilot vividly recalled to me how Beebe honored the implied contract between Delta employees and management that a loyal, productive employee would have a job for life.

During the 1974 fuel crisis [note that periodic fuel crises are simply part of life in the airline business], rather than lay off pilots Beebe offered them about 200 of them jobs on the ramp servicing Delta planes. Although some pilots considered this demeaning, the decision made sense for Delta because the company avoided paying employees for not working and for the pilots because they kept a job and seniority with Delta until the economy improved and they could go back to flying

During Beebe's tenure, in 1972 Delta merged with Northeast Airlines, providing routes from Florida to the Northeast part of the country.

Beebe sets the stage for protégé Allen to later become CEO

Beebe's main long-term effect on Delta was his insistence that Ron Allen become CEO. Beebe liked Allen and mentored him almost from the time Allen joined the company. Beebe insured that Allen would be next in line for CEO after Garrett.

The Davis book says that Allen was "...purely and simply Beebe's creature and it was something he was proud of." As the next chapter demonstrates, Allen may have been a loyal Delta employee and a satisfactory executive, but he was a poor choice for CEO. Davis further said, after Allen was made a vice president long before Delta would normally have done that, "It was no secret any longer; Allen was Beebe's protégé and was on a fast track that would, eventually, stampede Allen's career interests over those of such long-term senior company executives as Dick Maurer, Bob Oppenlander and Hollis Harris."

Davis said he had "become increasingly uneasy in the presence of Messrs. Beebe and Allen, with their unyielding way of second guessing decisions made by staff professionals as well as operations people. Then, too, I viewed them as intellectually dishonest men, fickle in their judgments and capricious in their decisions..."

Comments from interviewees who knew Allen well are consistent with the above comments. Allen must have adopted the apparent arrogance of Beebe, because it was a typical part of his behavior after he later became CEO.

If the many details about Beebe in the Davis book are correct, then making Beebe CEO was Delta's 7th

9/11. This was the first time, but not the last, that loyal, professional Delta people had to overcome a harmful action by the CEO.

Garrett CEO from 1978 - 1987

Beebe's health problems required him to step down and Dave Garrett took over as CEO in 1978.

After three decades of profitable years, in the early 1980's, Delta ran into difficult financial waters resulting from the double-digit inflation and high fuel costs under President Carter.

Delta employees, in what many still consider one of the most remarkable demonstrations of employee loyalty in American business history, bought a plane for the company. In an employee-initiated, volunteer effort, employees raised $30 million in payroll deductions to purchase Delta's first Boeing 767, named the "The Spirit of Delta."

Another example of the employee loyalty during this period is the extra effort flight crews often made at less used airports where Delta contracted the ground work to third parties. Pilots and flight attendants, if necessary, would get off the plane to make sure baggage was loaded and the plane properly prepared to fly.

A retired Delta employee said, "Mr. Garret was a 'regular guy' who was both smart and lucky. He would come down and walk around the ramp, where he knew the people on it. He would visit at 5 a.m. instead of during business hours like most executives would do."

Under Garrett, Delta revenues, operating profit and net profit doubled.

"We Love To Fly And It Shows" Campaign

One of the first things that occurred after Ron Allen became CEO in 1987 was the introduction of Delta's 'We Love To Fly And It Shows'™ advertising campaign.

Since the campaign ran on Allen's watch, he received the credit. However, the concept and development actually began a year earlier while David Garrett was CEO.

This theme and campaign captured in a contemporary style and words Mr. Woolman's customer focused and employee focused **'Service And Hospitality From The Heart'** philosophy on which the company was built.

In an audiocassette tape given to employees in September 1987 to announce the upcoming campaign, Whit Hawkins conveyed the substance and truth behind the campaign. Hawkins said,

"For as long as I have been working for Delta, we've had a saying, **'All airlines are alike, only people make them different'**. I don't know of any saying that has more lasting value than that. So when we are talking about advertising or marketing this company, we really need to show what makes this company and that's the people. Therefore any campaign that we do, to be effective, I believe has to evolve and revolve around the people of the company."

The campaign was the largest Delta had ever run up to that point. It ran in print, on television and on radio. The radio commercial ran on over 600 stations with over 210 million listener impressions a week.

TV commercials using Delta employees

The television commercials showed real Delta employees happily serving customers in situations that had actually occurred.

The one I still remember vividly was the Delta ticket agent sprinting down the corridor to return a briefcase to an on board passenger who had left it at the ticket counter.

The London Philharmonic performed the robust score supporting these still powerful lyrics:

"There's a difference when you're flying

With someone who's really trying

Someone who shows how much they care

Someone who makes it look so easy

Someone who's really glad you're there

Delta

We love to fly and the feeling grows

We love to fly and it shows

Delta

We love to fly and the feeling grows

We love to fly and it shows"

Note: The above lyrics are © 1987 Delta Air Lines, Inc.

We Love To Fly And It Shows is a registered trademark of Delta Air Lines, Inc.

The campaign was and is a poignant reminder of Mr. Woolman's leadership until 1966 and the long shadow he has continued to cast on the company. It is also a testimony to the employees and the leadership immediately following him. Unfortunately, the Woolman shadow began to diminish in earnest during the 10 years Allen was CEO.

Woolman-trained CFO

In addition to loyal, professional Delta employees, Bob Oppenlander was the constant during the time of these three CEO's. He was very instrumental in Delta's success during the time of maturation.

He was successful in shepherding Delta financially through the move to an all jet fleet and the initial significant international expansion.

Oppenlander also helped engineer the successful merger with Western Airlines in 1987 shortly before his retirement.

Mr. Woolman had brought in Oppenlander as Controller from consultant Cresap, McCormick & Paget. Upon retirement of the CFO several years after Oppenlander's arrival, he was promoted to that position.

For three decades, Oppenlander kept a firm and steady hand on the finances of Delta. He earned deep respect from within and outside the company.

He served effectively in a variety of circumstances and under four different CEO's – Woolman, Dolson, Beebe and Garrett.

During his tenure, the company successfully met the challenges of external circumstances like the Viet Nam war, hyperinflation and a recession.

He was an integral part of the management team that profitably converted Delta into an all jet airline.

Oppenlander graduated from Massachusetts Institute of Technology with a degree in management and earned an MBA at Harvard Business School.

His educational and professional background belies the myth held by Mullin's team and others that Delta was run by a bunch of "backwoods country bumpkins."

Impressive financial results

In the 21 years from 1966 to 1987, Delta achieved the following financial and operating milestones:

- Annual operating revenues increased 16 2/3 times from $319 million to $5.3 billion
- Annual operating profits increased over 6 times from $66 million to $405 million
- Total assets increased over 17 times from $314 million to $5.3 billion
- Shareholders equity increased over 15½ times from $124 million to $1.9 billion
- Revenue passenger miles increased over 71/2 times from 5.0 million to 38.4 million
- Revenue passengers increased over 6 ¼ times from 7.6 million to 48.2 million

Delta's 2nd 9/11 - Deregulation

The second 9/11 for Delta was 1978 when the Airline Deregulation Act passed Congress.

Some pundits have been highly critical of the Delta management and Board for not reacting strongly and quickly enough to the potential threat posed by deregulation and the eventually inevitable low cost carrier presence.

While their point has some merit, the context of the situation makes their non-reaction understandable.

Delta management had a growing, financially successful airline based in one of the country's most rapidly growing areas and mediocre competition.

Delta's primary competition continued to be Eastern, an airline beset with spotty customer service, poor labor/management relations and financial difficulties. (Eastern eventually closed its doors on January 18, 1991.)

As a result, the Board and Delta management, while continuing to talk about deregulation and low-cost carriers for years, apparently saw no need to make a strategic response.

This lack of concern culminated quite naturally in the Board eventually making Ron Allen CEO. No one I interviewed ever believed Allen had skills as a strategist. The Board did not think the company needed one.

Woolman shadow dims but survives

During this 21-year period when Delta matured as a company, Mr. Woolman's legacy survived. It dimmed during the Beebe tenure, but revived under Garrett.

At this point, Delta has survived its first two 9/11's – Woolman's death and deregulation - and continues to prosper. Then Delta faced its 3rd 9/11 - a midlife crisis with a CEO many thought should not have had the job.

5 – Delta's Midlife Crisis

How Ron Allen became CEO

"Tom Beebe." – Response of interviewees when asked how Ron Allen (in his mid-40's and 24 years after he joined the company) was selected as CEO and his qualifications for the job.

Notable quotes

"Every man who takes office either grows or swells, and when I give a man an office, I watch him carefully to see whether he is swelling or growing." **Thomas Woodrow Wilson**

"Ron's problem was he started believing in his own PR." – Interviewee

"Ron Allen had an ego as big as any pilots, probably larger." – Retired pilot interviewee

"Experience teaches only the teachable." - Aldous Huxley

Delta's 3rd 9/11 – Allen not a captain

In an airplane, the captain is in charge of the ship. The first officer is his or her second in command. Both are well trained and have important roles. However, the captain has more experience and has demonstrated over time the ability to carry out that huge responsibility for lives and expensive equipment.

Based on all the evidence, particularly the experience of interviewees, it is fair to say that Ron Allen may have been satisfactory as a first officer, but the Board should not have made him captain of Delta Air Lines.

It is also fair to say that Allen had a solid management team along the tens of thousands of long-standing loyal, professional Delta employees.

The observations about Allen in this book are intended to fall squarely only on his shoulders and not on the management team members or Delta employees.

Before Allen became CEO and after he left, that management team and the employees demonstrated their ability to run a fine airline.

For example, employees working under Allen's senior management team ran the airline successfully for the first three years after Allen left in 1997 and before Leo Mullin, who knew nothing about the airline business, brought in the management outsiders who nearly destroyed the business.

Delta's problem during the Allen decade was the top leader that the Board selected.

Allen joined Delta in 1963 upon graduation from Georgia Tech. His entire working life was at Delta.

Mr. Woolman was still in charge of the company when Allen joined it. However, Woolman's declining health and his death three years later deprived Allen of the opportunity to understudy the founder over an extended period as his 3 predecessors had done.

Allen was blessed with a smart, experienced executive team in Maurice Worth, Bob Coggin, Harry Alger and Tom Roeck.

He was also blessed to have a company with tens of thousands of committed employees and loyal customers. Delta was a profitable company with a bright future. In sports parlance, it was Allen's game to lose.

The Woolman shadow faded significantly, but did not disappear, under Allen's tenure.

However, Allen becoming CEO was the first tipping point in Delta employee/management relations from which the company has yet to recover.

Choice of the boss is not a succession plan

Ron Allen is reportedly a smart, energetic man with a strong work ethic. He makes a good first impression and can be quite articulate on his feet. He frequently professed his love for Delta, although he was often unable to translate that love in ways that benefited the company.

Presumably, he contributed to the company or he wouldn't have been allowed to stay and rise to the Chief Operating Officer position.

However, Allen's youth, attitude and management style arguably made him a candidate for CEO with a low probability for success.

Many interviewees, both inside and outside the company, questioned his appointment when it was made.

Looking back, the kindest statement I heard about his performance was "the job just got too big for Ron". Another said he "could do a great job running a company like [the size of] AirTran [which is much smaller than Delta]."

Succession planning the proper way

Succession planning in its simplest form identifies the skills, background and values required for a position. Then it determines if there is a potential match for that job with someone in the company.

Often there is someone but they need additional training or coaching to be prepared to assume the position and the company provides it. If there is no one who has the potential, then the next step is to bring someone in from the outside who meets the criteria or who can be groomed to meet them. The estimated timing of when the person currently in the position will move on helps determine the speed of these latter steps.

Viable CEO candidates passed over

From the interviews and other evidence, it appears there were at least three alternate candidates passed over in favor of Allen:

Hollis Harris, VP of In-Flight Service, who was a long-time Delta executive

Robert Oppenlander, Senior VP, Chief Financial Officer, who was a 30 year Delta executive and long-time CFO

Gerald Grinstein, CEO of Western Airlines prior to its acquisition by Delta in 1987

Based on what I have learned, any of these three seem more likely to have been qualified than Allen for the CEO position.

There was wide respect for *Hollis Harris* among front-line troops and the executive team. Many were very disappointed when Harris was not selected because they believed he was clearly the best-qualified candidate and the one who had the most support throughout the organization.

Their assessment of Harris' CEO qualifications was accurate. Harris had two successful stints as a CEO when he left Delta after serving as COO under Allen for a time.

The first was as CEO of Air Canada, which he successfully led during a difficult time of transition from a government run airline to a private business.

Then Harris became CEO of World Airways. He returned to profitability this charter air carrier, now based near the Atlanta airport. Harris retired last year at the age of 72 having created a succession plan that left World Airways (now World Air) in the hands of a capable successor CEO and leadership team.

The Aviation Hall of Fame inducted Harris (and "Pre" Ball, Delta's chief pilot under Dolson) in 2005.

Bob Oppenlander was a modest, self-effacing man. He was nearing retirement age and was looking forward to being home with his wife and playing golf more often. I had the pleasure of playing golf with him on several occasions.

The situation would have required a tough fight for anyone other than Allen to be elected CEO by the Board. It is likely Oppenlander was unwilling to go through the tough political fight. He asked that his name be taken out of consideration.

Gerald Grinstein became part of the Delta family in 1987 when Delta acquired Western Air Lines. Grinstein led the team that successfully restored Western to financial health.

There was reportedly at least one discussion in which Garrett offered the Delta CEO job Grinstein. Grinstein declined because he thought Western people needed to understand they were part of Delta and needed to adapt to its culture. He was concerned that his appointment would send a mixed message.

The reader can speculate on how different Delta might be today were any of these men named Delta CEO in 1987 instead of Allen.

I believe that the exact same management team (including Allen) and employees that were under Allen, with a different, more effective leader as CEO, would have avoided or minimized the problems Delta faced. There would have been no Leo Mullin and a company far less likely to be facing imminent bankruptcy today.

Perceptions of Ron Allen

Along with the good characteristics possessed by Allen, others made him a leader of questionable effectiveness.

Some perceived Allen as a spendthrift. A long-time employee said, "Money was flying out the door [under Allen]."

One former Pan Am employee said they were shocked when they saw "money walking out the door" when they first visited Delta's General Offices shortly after Delta acquired the Pan Am assets in 1991.

After the Pan Am asset acquisition, Allen retained millions of dollars of unused real estate interests around the world, unnecessarily tying up capital and adding to expenses.

Exacerbating the problem, Allen sidelined CFO Tom Roeck from effective participation in major decisions by excluding him from his Executive Council.

It is hard to understand why the Board tolerated this exclusion of the Delta CFO, given the capital-intensive nature of the business and the ongoing discussions about critical financial decisions – like the Pan Am asset acquisition - being made at the time

Midlife Crisis

With a marginalized CFO, a laissez faire Board and an intimidating manner that generally prevented employees from expressing financial concerns, Allen had little or no financial oversight. The result was that Allen spent typically money on what he wanted whenever he chose.

The above scenario set the stage for four consecutive years (FY 1991 – FY 1994) of operating losses totaling over $2.0 *billion*.

Other than the temporary financial setbacks under Garrett in the early 1980's, this period was the first time Delta had lost money in over 40 years.

Allen acted as if he expected employees to serve him instead of serving them so they could effectively serve the customer. This is in stark contrast to Mr. Woolman's servant leadership approach. Allen must have understood Mr. Woolman, but that did not translate over to following his methods. Allen was the "opposite of a servant heart". He became "imperial" in the words of one.

One interviewee, a former long-time Delta employee, said about Allen, "When he took over the company started to change. He was a different type of leader than Mr. Woolman. For Allen, it was more about him being served than him providing for employees to take care of customers."

Eventually Allen began *"believing his own PR"*, demonstrating behavior that indicated a view the company would not survive without him.

Allen was perceived as arrogant (a word used by many interviewees). He often acted as if he knew all the answers and other executives and employees knew nothing.

This arrogance transferred over to his relationship with the Board and surely affected their decision to terminate him. Allen was so out of touch with the reality of the situation that, reportedly, when the Board told him of their decision to terminate him, it was a complete surprise.

This arrogance combined with the appearance of a closed mind and a disregard for Delta people. People who have presented to him report an attitude of "my (Allen's) way or the highway" if he disagreed with what the presenter had to say.

Although Allen had been head of personnel, he "didn't understand the employees", in the words of one interviewee, any more than Leo Mullin the outsider who was brought in after Allen.

Everyone at Delta was on the same team under Woolman's leadership and his values. There truly was a "Delta family."

When there was a problem, management and employees accepted joint responsibility for the problem and for fixing it. As one interviewee said, "We always knew that we could count on everybody looking out for each other."

Allen's behavior created a perception that the team no longer existed.

Allen did not display the skills to engage employees in a way that would help reinforce their proprietary good feeling for Delta. He frequently insulted or was derogatory toward others, including his senior officers, in public. One interviewee saw him reduce a senior officer to tears, fully visible to all attendees, in the middle of a room at a break in a large meeting.

Understandably, some executives and managers at headquarters made an ongoing, conscious effort to stay out of Allen's sight to avoid having to deal with him.

Allen also demonstrated childish behavior, pitching temper tantrums and throwing papers at other executives, frustrating and embarrassing them.

Leader temperament: Board responsibility

We hear a lot about 'judicial temperament' when Congress debates nominees for the Federal Judiciary.

Similarly, an effective leader must have the right temperament to run the organization they are responsible for leading. This means it is the Board's responsibility to make sure they select a CEO with *the proper temperament for their particular organization.*

It is difficult to understand how the Delta Board did not know intimately Allen's temperament and how contrary it was to the temperament that was best suited for the job of Delta CEO.

The Board had many opportunities to observe Allen during his years as Delta President under Garrett. The behavioral characteristics and attitudes he displayed, which seriously hampered if not prevented his effectiveness, did not miraculously appear overnight once he was elected CEO.

Presumably, the Board also should have known about the unfavorable perceptions of Allen held by many of the other leaders and employees.

My experience and that of many others confirms that people rarely change their temperament; if they do, it is only after making a conscious commitment to change and a huge, ongoing effort to do it.

It should not have been surprising to anyone that Allen was highly unlikely to change. After all, he was Beebe's anointed one and, therefore, had no incentive or need to change one iota in order to get the CEO job.

A plausible explanation for the Board's action is they felt intimidated or overshadowed by Beebe.

In addition, it appears that at the time of Allen's election and for years afterward, the Board was comprised of many members of the 'old school' who were perfectly content to go along with management.

Interviewees cited specific examples demonstrating how some of these Board members were disengaged from the issues facing Delta.

A well-known Board member frequently would lean over to ask a senior Delta executive, in Board meetings, questions that indicated a lack of understanding of the issues and facts.

When the Board terminated Allen in 1997, one long-time Board member called a Delta executive to ask, "Why did we fire Ron?"

Ron Allen's amorphous goals

Ron Allen came into Delta and promptly announced his amorphous goal for Delta was to be "the most respected airline in the world."

Allen modified this goal, in the 1991 annual report, to one equally amorphous - become "one of the world's prominent airlines." Allen's letter to shareholders cited this goal as the justification for the purchase of the Pan Am assets that year.

As events unfolded, it became clear both these goals were a reflection of Allen's large ego and lack of strategic ability rather than a realistic objective.

Strategic Planning 101 teaches that effective business goals must meet three criteria:

- Specific

- Measurable

- Achievable

Allen's goals met none of these criteria. As a result, the company was put in a position where business decisions were made in a strategic vacuum. Allen's wishes and whims filled the vacuum. This proved true throughout his tenure according to those familiar with the situation.

Purchase of Pan Am assets

Jim Collins, author of the best selling book "Good To Great," said in the March 21, 2005 issue of *Fortune* magazine, "The real discipline comes in saying no to the wrong opportunities."

Billionaire Ed Ball, former head of Florida East Coast Railway and executor to the estate of one of the Dupont heirs, often said, "A businessperson should never have to buy or have to sell." His point, of course, was to manage your business in such a way that it was never essential to do any deal, no matter how desirable it may be. It was also a caution never to want a deal so badly that the businessperson was willing to pay any price to do it.

Pros and cons of Pan Am asset purchase

There are both pro and con opinions about Ron Allen's decision to purchase the Pan Am assets.

The rationale at the time was to elevate more quickly Delta's international presence, immediately giving it multiple routes and moving the perception of Delta from a regional airline to a major player in the industry.

While the Pan Am deal was a key factor in the 4 consecutive years of losses for Delta, 14 years later the company is benefiting from it. Today Delta's international routes are profitable and Delta, as a result, is now adding international destinations, while trimming the unprofitable domestic routes. While Allen's deal cost Delta dearly, it is helping the company survive today.

Too little due diligence and too high a price

Some Delta people present at the time believe he wanted the deal so badly he neglected to do adequate due diligence that would have uncovered more accurately the value of the underlying assets and the costs to make them productive and, partly as a result, he overpaid.

As interviewees repeatedly pointed out, his Pan Am asset purchase in 1991 set the stage for Delta's financial problems in the first place.

There is a perception that Allen paid far too much for those assets – perhaps driven by personal and corporate ego and by perceiving Delta was in a bidding war with Carl Icahn of TWA.

Also, knowledgeable interviewees believe Allen wanted the Pan Am assets so badly that he overlooked predictable serious cost, integration and cultural issues that were to result from the purchase and contribute significantly to Delta's years of loss following the asset purchase.

Known Pan Am maintenance problems ignored

Delta people had concerns about known maintenance problems with the Pan Am equipment. Allen discounted or overlooked these problems.

As a long-time Delta executive, Chief Operating Officer and Board member, before becoming CEO, Allen was in a position where he must have been aware of these problems.

Instead, he later publicly blamed his maintenance people and others for failing to inform him of the issues, accepting no responsibility himself.

Delta had previously had an interchange agreement with Pan Am in Miami (Pan Am people would fly one of their planes to Miami and then turn the plane over to Delta people there to fly to the next domestic destination.).

Reportedly, while that agreement was in effect, Delta operations people frequently encountered cabin maintenance problems on Pan Am aircraft that reflected maintenance standards well below those of Delta. Similar airworthiness problems were reportedly encountered and Delta mechanics had to fix these Pan Am plane problems too before they would fly the plane. From that experience, Delta knew that Pan Am's maintenance quality was not up to Delta's standards.

Predictable Pan Am maintenance problems happened

In addition, Pan Am was in financial trouble for years before the Delta purchase. Common sense would indicate that their maintenance would have suffered and predict that former Pan Am planes would require costly maintenance work by Delta after the purchase. This happened.

Aircraft have a unique alphanumeric designation. Delta people gave one former Pan Am aircraft – easily recognized by its number – the name "Christine" after it became widely known the aircraft frequently created flight delays due to maintenance problems.

Another predictable, but costly, post-purchase maintenance problem was that former Pan Am aircraft had bastardized parts. These planes were called PUD's (acronym for Pan Am, United and Delta) since they had parts from the three different airlines that owned the aircraft at different times.

Pan Am facilities problems

In pushing through the asset purchase Allen apparently focused on the routes and aircraft involved in the deal while overlooking the practicalities of implementing the purchase.

Delta reportedly did not negotiate for some of the obvious Pan Am owned facilities needed to support the purchased assets. For example, after the purchase, it was discovered that Delta had not negotiated to acquire the employee parking lot in New York City so flight attendants would have a place to park while on a trip.

The purchased Pan Am facilities required a huge effort and expense to repair. One interviewee described them as a "money pit."

Leadership 7.5 – Contract with employees is broken

After the 4 years of losses under his leadership, Allen and the Board finally recognized the need to cut costs.

However, he must bear primary responsibility, along with the Board, for putting Delta in a position, or allowing it to get there, where drastic cost cuts were a necessity.

Goal never achieved but profitability returned

The goal of Leadership 7.5 was to reduce Delta's Cost per Available Seat Mile (CASM), a commonly used airline industry metric for unit cost, to 7.5¢ down from 9.4¢ a mile in the fiscal year ending June 30, 1994, the fourth of four consecutive years of losses totaling $2.0 billion for the company.

In an attempt to reach this goal, Delta laid off approximately 3,000 workers and thousands more accepted Delta's offer of early retirement or other voluntary programs. During fiscal year 1995, almost 10,000 people left Delta – a 14% reduction from the 69,555 employees a year earlier.

In addition, the company took steps that impacted customer service in ways visible to the customer, who had come to expect quality service from Delta. For example, Delta's frequent flyer plan was scaled back, meals were eliminated on shorter flights and the company reduced the number of flight attendants on a plane. Delta's contract with customers was broken along with the contract with employees.

After four years of a negative spread between CASM and Revenue Per Available Seat Mile (RASM), which meant that Delta lost money for every Available Seat Mile it flew, in fiscal 1995 the spread turned positive by 50¢. As a result, Delta once again was profitable.

The CASM was 8.83¢ in FY 1995, 9.17¢ in FY 1996 and 8.82¢ in FY 1997, Allen's last year as CEO.

The financial community took notice of the progress. For example, on March 27, 1997 (dated after he had been informed of his impending termination on June 30, 1997), Ron Allen sent a memorandum to the Board and copied Officers and Directors. He noted an attached report from Glenn Engle of Goldman Sachs that said, "We regard Delta, which is on our U.S. priority list, as the most attractive airline stock in the world."

Two part contract is broken

The steps taken to make those drastic cuts broke Delta's long established, implicit contract with employees that had two important elements:

Their jobs were secure. In the past, when Delta's finances were tight, management would retain employees anyway. The company would do this even if it meant putting some to work temporarily performing a job different from their primary one.

Serving the customer well was part of Delta's DNA. This was the daily focus of everyone in the airline, from top to bottom. Whenever belt tightening was necessary, the team figured out ways to do it that prevented or minimized the impact on the customer. Everyone in the "Delta family" took pride in being a part of delivering quality service.

Leadership 7.5 cost Delta dearly. There were dramatic losses in employee morale and loyalty. The inevitable result was losses in customer satisfaction and loyalty. Common sense and experience, along with Mr. Woolman's lessons, dictates that unhappy employees = unhappy customers.

After 16 years of being the #1 airline in customer satisfaction, Delta slipped from the top rung.

The result was a negative impact on employee / management relations at the company that persists to a degree today.

As one interviewee put it, "Under Allen, the trust [in management] had gone."

Manner of employee cuts hurt morale

It was clear to most everyone at the time, both inside and outside of Delta, that cuts were necessary to keep the company viable.

However, the focus on costs was almost exclusive, effectively overshadowing concern about Delta people.

Prior to 7.5, Delta employees looked out for each other. If an employee had a problem, it generally was addressed in a respectful and caring manner by a supervisor or manager. The employee was most often given the opportunity to correct the problem.

While management intended to treat employees humanely and, in general, made policy decisions in keeping with that intention, the story was often different at lower levels.

Almost overnight, the company began putting some people in supervisory and management positions that consistently demonstrated a lack of concern for either employee or the customer.

Lack of accountability had often been an issue at Delta through the years, attributed by some to the "Delta family" culture.

This lack of accountability now resulted in free rein for those many considered were highly political or abusive managers. These managers favored and promoted like-minded employees; they ran rough shod over more gracious and caring Delta people.

For example, one interviewee told me a chilling story of the day the cost-cutting plan was presented to headquarters employees in their division. The story is an early indication of the decline in the mutual respect and support among Delta employees that began during the implementation of Leadership 7.5.

A long-time "Delta family" member joined a large group to watch a PowerPoint presentation about a restructure in their division from 7.5. Only then did they learn that their job was being eliminated.

In a conference with their supervisor following the general meeting, the employee, who had never received an unfavorable review or coaching on needed improvements, was unable to get a definitive answer to the question why they lost their job.

To add insult to injury, although their performance had been appraised favorably for years, they were told that those whose jobs were eliminated must interview for a possible job in the restructured organization. The criteria for selection were never clear.

Restructures du jour and programs du jour begin

From Leadership 7.5 forward until Gerald Grinstein took over in 2004, Delta was in a constant state of flux resulting from ongoing restructures, new programs and temporary initiatives.

This created an environment throughout the organization where the ability to suggest seemingly creative ideas in a meeting and initiating high profile projects were often more highly regarded than proven management skills considered valuable before.

Encouraged by a coterie of expensive consultants (particularly the one which guided Leadership 7.5), deriving handsome fees to assist in the projects, these new 'leaders' leveraged their increased visibility into promotions and raises.

Fortunately, most of those 'leaders' are gone from Delta; yet a few remain. Delta can ill afford them now.

Consultant's cookie cutter approach the foundation of negative long-term result from 7.5

Delta had never previously faced a financial crisis of the magnitude faced in 1994.

Due to the size of the problem, management determined substantial cuts would be necessary. Delta had no experience in doing that.

Therefore, to assist him, Allen engaged a large, well-known management-consulting firm that had satisfactorily completed one limited engagement for the company. [This book refers to that firm as "*Consultant X*". No name is used because the focus is on Delta management and their responsibility in selecting and managing the consulting firm. In addition, that firm's approach is generally similar enough to other large management consulting firms that the names could be considered interchangeable.]

On several occasions, I have consulted with clients at the same time as *Consultant X* was consulting with them on other engagements. In addition, I have made it a habit to remain aware of the practices of other firms. As part of this effort, I frequently ask business leaders about their experience and satisfaction with other consulting firms.

My experiences with *Consultant X* and those of many with whom I have spoken have often not been favorable. Yet this firm, like other large management consulting firms, has established a brand among Boards and top management, who continue to hire them and recommend these firms to others at their level.

For example, early in the life of my firm, one client was a *Fortune* 100 company. Since the inception of the business, clients have repeatedly told me that my 4 – 6 page letter proposals are clear, comprehensive communications that effectively establish mutual expectations. If the client agrees, they initial and date the proposal and we start work.

After several engagements working on that basis with this particular client, the next proposal was returned to me with a 40+-page contract to replace it. I learned that there had been a *$1 million cost overrun*, which the contract required be paid, on a project the client had with *Consultant X*. As a result, management issued the edict to make sure *Consultant X* would never be in a position again to repeat that behavior. The rest of us were tarnished with that same dirty brush.

The approach *Consultant X* followed with Delta on Leadership 7.5 was very similar, if not identical, to the approach they followed at another mutual client around the same time.

In a nutshell, in both cases, they facilitated management's determination of the 'straw man' – the total desired cost savings on the project – for the company.

A senior executive who has worked directly with them told me the process of *Consultant X* works like this:

- In their marketing approach, to sell the engagement initially, they provide the prospective client with cost numbers for others in their same industry and then show them their costs are out of line. This enables *Consultant X* then to promise they will earn their fee by helping the client bring their costs in line with the 'averages'.

- On the surface, this proposition sounds too good to ignore, particularly for a company that was 'on the ropes' financially as Delta was at the time.

- Unfortunately, since the approach focuses management and the consultant exclusively on cost savings, it ignores the potential long-term costs of following that approach.

- Specifically, the one-dimensional approach minimizes or ignores the human factors involved in cost cutting.

- While this oversight is significant in any organization, at Delta, which built its business on employee satisfaction = customer satisfaction, it proved to be extremely harmful to the company, with negative effects that last to this day.

- Once management determines the corporate 'straw man', then teams are formed for specific areas of the company to develop a 'straw man' for each area and plans to cuts costs to knock it down. The intent is for this process to, collectively, enable achievement of the corporate goal.

- *Consultant X* assigns a junior member of their engagement team to each team to monitor the team's progress and attend all meetings. The monitor reports back to the engagement manager as needed.

- Unbeknownst to many clients, the monitor often has a substantial incentive to achieve cost savings greater than necessary to meet the client's corporate goal. Therefore, the monitor will be likely to push the team to keep looking for savings well beyond where it is prudent.

- The pressure on the monitors to produce extra cost savings is the result of *Consultant X*'s contract with the client providing a bonus above the fee if incremental savings above the corporate 'straw man' are produced.

In my opinion, this approach places the consulting firm and the engagement team in a potential conflict of interest position. They face ongoing ethical dilemmas from the financial incentive. One possible result would be leading the client to make decisions and take actions potentially detrimental to the client's long-term interests.

There are three leadership lessons here:

- When engaging a consultant a leader should be sure the engagement agreement is one where the consultant's only incentive is to provide advice in the client's best interests

- When a leader needs a consultant and is inexperienced in using one, seek independent advice from a consultant with no financial stake in the outcome to provide guidance in the proposal and negotiation stages and, if needed, during the actual engagement

- The leader must exert their responsibility to check the premises behind a consultant's proposal to insure it takes into consideration all the factors the company needs the engagement to address, not just the one that is easiest for the consultant to help attain.

Consultant X gets an annuity

Ron Allen became dependent on *Consultant X* during Leadership 7.5. He put them on retainer, just to be available to him, at a reported $1 million a month fee.

In addition, *Consultant X* was given carte blanche to stay at Delta permanently looking for subsequent work.

This permission created the perception that *Consultant X* was the favorite of the boss and, therefore, smart company politics to use them as much and as often as possible.

Delta managers used them frequently, generating what would likely be hundreds of thousand of dollars in additional consultant fees from a client struggling to return to profitability.

One retired long-time Delta manager said, "The invasion of [*Consultant X*] makes the invasion of the locusts look mild. Also, they (the consulting firm) never leave."

Their annuity continued under Leo Mullin, an alumnus of *Consultant X* whose main Delta contact had been a groomsman in Mullin's wedding.

To the silent applause of many people in the "Delta family," one of Gerald Grinstein's first acts when he took over as CEO in January 2004 was to cut off the annuity.

However, this did not last long; *Consultant X* was brought back into Delta, where I understand they remain to this day.

Post evaluation of Leadership 7.5

I have read a thorough and thoughtful review, prepared by a former senior Delta executive, of the Leadership 7.5 initiative. In general, I think the comments from most interviewees approximate this executive's views about Leadership 7.5, its effects on Delta and the lessons learned. By permission, these are highlights:

Positive effects of 7.5

- It caused many Delta people, especially in middle management to focus on inefficiencies and ways to improve them.

- Successful changes in travel agency commission structure gave Delta the courage to make other cost saving changes in the distribution process.

- Many actions were taken to address legacy cost inefficiencies.

- Overall the people in Delta became more cost conscious.

Lessons learned

- Don't wait until the "wolf is at the door" before addressing fundamental issues affecting the cost and efficiency of your enterprise. As a matter of principle, these need to be looked at all the time.

- Good cost efficiency must be balanced with customer service, but the company must never make the customer feel like they are carrying the entire burden for the cost reduction actions.

- If your company has a customer service culture, don't make the mistake of taking away the tools your front line personnel need to deliver good customer service. If you do take away many of the tools, you risk destroying that culture and in the end the customer pays the price.

- You can't take a hatchet to a customer facing function, such as the gate and ticket counter agents, and transition from experienced people to those with little or no experience and expect to continue delivering an acceptable level of service.

- Understand what success looks like and when to declare victory. About a year into 7.5, Delta's unit cost had become the best of any major airline and the company had again become profitable. However, to meet the expectations Delta had created with Wall Street, the company continued to painfully reduce costs as it worked toward the 7.5 "magic number."

- Insure that you have flexibility to adjust your targets up or down as business conditions change.

- You can't take a broad-brush approach to head count reductions. You have to understand the consequences of the actions you are about to take. (For example, so many experienced L1011 mechanics took early retirement that dispatch reliability of the plane seriously suffered.)

- When outsourcing a labor-intensive operation like cabin cleaning, the plan can't be implemented overnight. There must be a blend of experienced personnel working with the outsource crew for a period of time to produce satisfactory results.

- If customer input is sought related to their preferences for things like meals and services, be extremely careful in how questions are asked and their answers interpreted. Customers frequently fail to fully comprehend the full implications of your questions and the answers. Not taking appropriate care in 7.5 resulted in very serious customer relations problems regarding onboard service.

Specific regrets about 7.5

- Customers had to pay a high price for the actions taken during that period, some of which linger still today.

- Much of the Delta "Customer Service Culture" was lost as a result of the initiative.

- More extensive communications were needed across the company, particularly due to Delta's culture and the nature of the initiative.

- It did so much damage to the "Delta family".

Employee survey documents the 7.5 damage

The damage to the "Delta family" and the increased mistrust and lack of confidence in Allen was documented in the results of the 1996 Survey of Delta Personnel.

I have conducted and analyzed a considerable number of employee surveys in my work and reviewed the Delta results in the context of my experience.

When I first saw the published results in February 1997, my immediate reaction was "Allen is gone."

Negative results would be expected for an employee survey conducted immediately following a major cost cutting initiative like Leadership 7.5. However, these particular results appeared to me to be so strongly negative that no responsible Board could permit Allen to stay. He had completely lost the credibility with employees needed to lead Delta.

My second reaction was professional. In my opinion, any management consultant that organized and directed an enterprise-wide project that produced a long-term effect like that of 7.5 should be professionally embarrassed and ashamed at the damage suffered by their client.

The standard large consulting firm excuse that "We only suggested; the problem was in the client's implementation" just didn't cut it for me in the case of Delta.

It seemed to me that whatever firm was responsible had led a well meaning, but naïve top management down a path with predictable negative results.

Highlights of the survey results were:

- There was a significant difference in perceptions between management and non-management (90% of total respondents), with management across the board perceiving the company in a more favorable light.

- A review of these results confirms a significant mistrust of Delta's management and lack of respect for them by non-management Delta employees. For example, 50% of those respondents gave an unfavorable rating to the question, "How would you rate your company on effective leadership?"

- It is also noteworthy in a company built on a strong relationship between management and employees that 44% of non-management employees gave an unfavorable rating to the question, "How would you rate the company on taking a genuine interest in the well-being of Delta people?"

- When asked "How would you rate the extent to which you are treated by Senior Management with respect and dignity," 39% of non-management employees responded unfavorably. Non-management employees responded unfavorably 39% of the time to the question, "How would you rate the overall job done by Delta's senior management, as a group?"

Even though many interviewees considered Ron Allen primarily responsible for these and other negative employee perceptions, his top leadership team was painted with the same broad brush as a result of working for Allen.

Valuable Delta executives like Bob Coggin and Maurice Worth are known as fine people and appear to have done a good job through the years. However, these employee perceptions about "management" probably precluded them from consideration to replace Allen. Working for Allen was career limiting.

Financial results under Allen

Financially, looking only at the beginning of Allen's tenure in 1987 and comparing it to the end of it in 1997, he performed satisfactorily.

Financial highlights of Allen's time as CEO include:

- *Shareholders' Equity* increased from $1.9 to $3.0 billion – an increase of $1.1 billion or 58%.

- *Net Profit* rose from $264 million profit in 1987 to $845 million profit in 1997. This does not reflect the four years, under Allen's total 10 years as CEO, of cumulative net losses from FY 1991 to FY 1994 of almost $1.7 billion. Except for a brief time in the early 1980's, these were the first years Delta had lost money in decades.

Cumulatively during Allen's 10 years, the company's **net profit** was $712 million on combined **operating revenues** of $105.6 billion.

Cumulatively during the 10 years, the company's **operating profit** was $2.3 billion. This means the **overall operating margin** during that time was 2.1%.

The **spread between Operating Revenue per Available Seat Mile and the Operating Cost per Available Seat Mile** was favorable in the Allen's 6 years when the company made a profit. The spread was negative in each of the 4 years from 1991 to 1994 when the company was unprofitable.

Operating highlights include:

The **passenger load factor** (the % of total seats available filled with paying passengers) varied considerably under Allen. When he took over it was 55.7% and 74.1% when he left. In the intervening years, load factors ranged from 57.1% to 67.8% at FY end.

The **breakeven load factor** (the % of total seats available that must be filled to begin making a profit) increased from 51.1% to 62.7%, an increase of 22.7%.

The following **operating metrics** increased under Allen comparing 1997 results to those for 1987:

Revenue passengers – 110% increase

Revenue passenger miles – 155% increase

Available seat miles – 98% increase

The credit for these favorable results belongs primarily to the Delta people, not to their CEO.

A senior Delta executive, in a private letter to Gerald Grinstein dated June 13, 1997, said, "Many people inside and outside the company are very confused about Ron's departure in view of our excellent performance over the last few quarters. In reality, our strong performance has been significantly influenced by having a team of senior and middle level managers who have exercised a great deal of individual initiative to control or reduce cost, while improving the company's revenue performance."

Allen's departure performance

On the day of his departure as CEO, Allen propped his cowboy boot on the bumper of his car parked at Delta headquarters. He then strummed his guitar and sang a rendition of the country and western song, 'Mama, Don't Let Your Babies Grow up To Be Cowboys'. His audience was a small group of curious headquarters employees passing by on their way to other destinations.

Then Allen rode off from Delta into the sunset for the final time as a Delta employee and on to Coca-Cola to provide advice as a Board member of that company.

Allen's lucrative departure

Allen did not leave Delta for a life of poverty. Key elements of his termination package included:

- $4.5 million cash severance payment
- $500,000 annual "consulting" payment for 8 years – recently concluded for a total of $4,000,000
- $765,000 a year pension
- Multiple other perquisites valued at millions of dollars

Allen has received some public criticism about this arguably lavish package, particularly in light of Delta's financial woes. There have even been suggestions he give some of it back.

However, I believe anyone leveling criticism should instead address the Delta Board, particularly the Personnel and Compensation Committee that approved the package in the first place.

While Allen did do long-term damage to the company, Delta was back to profitability before he left.

His successor, along with the Delta Board, was the one who ultimately brought Delta to its knees.

Allen may have been treated far too well as he was ushered out the door, but he had no obligation to pay for later Board and management mistakes.

Assessment of Allen

A long-time frontline employee, when asked what he thought about Allen, said simply, "He was a failure."

I believe that is an overly harsh assessment.

Allen did do major, long-term damage to Delta.

He set the tone and made the decisions that led to the need for the Leadership 7.5 cost-cutting program.

As a result, he bears primary responsibility for damaging permanently Delta's unique, mutually beneficial contract with the "Delta family" and their trust and confidence that management would reward their loyalty with job security.

While his methods to restore profitability should be questioned, the fact remains the company was again profitable before the Board relieved him of his job.

Allen cared about Delta and its heritage. For example, he has consistently and actively supported the retirees who created and, in 1995, formally incorporated the Delta Air Transport Heritage Museum. The stated mission of the museum is, "Through the story of Delta Air Lines, its history and its people, the Museum preserves materials, interprets histories, discovers meanings, and explores the impacts of air transportation on technology, economic development, global events, and the personal lives of those touched by aviation."

The bottom line: Ron Allen was a loyal Delta employee who the Board promoted to a level higher than he was able to perform effectively.

Had Beebe not anointed Allen and he instead had to compete for the CEO job and earn it, I believe both the company and Allen would have benefited

Allen would have then found it necessary to face and address the limitations in his management ability. He would have remained a useful executive if he were unsuccessful; he might have made a satisfactory CEO were he successful in making needed behavior changes and developing his leadership knowledge and skills.

Instead, Delta now bears the scars of Allen's limitations and Allen must live with the knowledge many believe he permanently harmed the company where he spent his entire working life.

The lesson for any Board is to take a proactive stance in CEO selection, independently assume charge of the process and use all available tools and resources, not just the traditional ones.

By following this approach, a Board will greatly increase their chances of finding information that would indicate predictable, but undesirable performance of a CEO candidate. Using common sense, the Board will then be in a position to say no to a wrong candidate before they have subjected the organization and thousands of people to them.

At this point the "Delta family" has survived three 9/11's – Mr. Woolman's death, deregulation and Allen. Just ahead is Delta's fourth and most devastating 9/11 – Leo Mullin.

His 6½-year tenure can appropriately be described as an out-of-body experience for Delta's employees, customers and stockholders.

An out-of-body experience is the subjective perception that one is no longer in one's body, while (generally) being able to perceive it from the outside. It is sometimes associated with near-death experiences.

6 – Out-of-body Experience

Lame duck CEO creates pressure on Board

The Delta Board told Ron Allen it was over in early 1997, but allowed him to remain with the company until the summer. At the time they terminated him, the Board reportedly had no idea of who his replacement might be.

Under the duress of a lame duck CEO with no replacement in sight, the Board retained well-known Tom Neff of the executive search firm Spencer Stuart to help find a new CEO as quickly as possible.

Delta Board decides to find CEO outside

With the bad taste left from Allen's tenure among employees, management and Board, the Board's inclination was apparently to go outside the Delta family for the first time for the top job.

Because of the problems with Allen, the Board appears to have looked for a new CEO with the assumption that Delta was just too inbred to have produced a viable successor internally. Instead, they should have looked in the mirror and realized the problem was not inbreeding, but that they had simply picked the wrong internal candidate in 1987.

They found former management consultant Leo Mullin in the banking and utility businesses in Chicago. The Board hired Mullin in August 1997, passing over other obvious internal candidates – senior executives Maurice Worth, Bob Coggin and Harry Alger.

Each of these executives remained in their roles, reporting to Mullin, for a year or more after Mullin's arrival. They continued to perform effectively as they had under Allen.

Delta employees and this management team continued to run the airline successfully while Mullin began trying to learn a new industry and a new company.

Notable quotes

- "Leadership is doing what is right when no one is watching." – Unknown
- "Leadership is a combination of strategy and character. If you must be without one, be without the strategy." – Gen. H. Norman Schwarzkopf (Ret.)
- "It requires wisdom to understand wisdom: the music is nothing if the audience is deaf." - Walter Lippman
- "Who you are speaks so loudly I can't hear what you are saying." – Emerson
- "To build may have to be the slow and laborious task of years. To destroy can be the thoughtless act of a single day." – Winston Churchill
- "Be careful what you pray for; you might get it." - Unknown

Mullin hire – Delta's fourth 9/11

This decision became Delta's fourth 9/11. While dedicated, professional Delta people made sure the company survived and moved on from the first three, this 4th 9/11 has proved to be nearly fatal for the company.

In a battle of words in the July 25, 2005 issue of *Fortune*, Neff's archrival Gerry Roche of Heidrick & Struggles said, "If Tom considers Delta (placing Leo Mullin there in 1997) a success, he's smoking something."

The Delta Board, by appointing Mullin to be the CEO, was unfortunately behaving like the country and western song – "Looking For Love In All The Wrong Places."

A current Delta Board member once told me over lunch, in a discussion about companies with strong tradition bringing in a top executive from outside the company, that these people are merely, "hired guns that stay for a while and then move on."

What they did not say is that some of these hired guns, like Mullin, and their sidekicks clean out the bank and then shoot up the town quite badly before they leave it.

If this Board member's 'hired gun' mentality reflects that of the others, then preserving the Delta culture in bankruptcy will get no support from the Board.

In genetics and CEO's, make sure the outcross improves the species

In genetics, continued inbreeding is a key strategy to enhance and lock in the desired characteristics of a species. After a number of generations of continued inbreeding at some point, however, inbreeding also enhances one or more negative characteristics and suggests an outcross to a different genetic line.

The purpose of an outcross is to strengthen the species. The difficulty when outcrossing is deciding when and where you go to provide the outcross. The wrong outcross may dilute the previous accomplishments and in fact weaken the species.

Delta's 'promote from within' policy had reinforced the successful Woolman values and culture.

However, Allen was arguably the result of too much inbreeding at Delta with the negative results to show for it.

Therefore, it is understandable why the Board decided to go outside the company for a CEO - in effect to find an outcross - for the first time in history to replace Allen.

There was clearly a sour taste about management in employees' mouths, particularly because of the Leadership 7.5 mammoth cost cutting initiative.

In business, when bringing in new blood, the Board must make sure outcross improves the species

The cultural, human and financial results of Leo Mullin's 6 ½ year tenure at Delta clearly shows the Board, with the CEO search reportedly initiated and led by Board member and now CEO Gerald Grinstein, made a poor choice for an outcross.

Mullin credentials show low probability for success as CEO

Credentials are no guarantee of success – particularly if a Board looks at the wrong ones

It is not hindsight to observe that Mullin was the wrong man for the job. Both his background and behavioral characteristics strongly indicated this.

Out-of-body Experience

I believe it was predictable that the probability of success for Leo Mullin as CEO Delta was quite low.

Leo Mullin is widely considered a very smart man. He has three degrees from Harvard: undergraduate in engineering and applied physics; graduate degree in applied mathematics; MBA.

Yet being smart and knowing how to manipulate numbers do not translate directly into being able to manage successfully a large, global enterprise.

He was an executive with First Chicago Bank for 15 years, the last two of which was as Chief Operating Officer. In only two of those 15 years did he have a CEO position; from 1991 to 1993, he was CEO of a subsidiary bank. First Chicago Bank later merged with Banc One to form Bank One. J.P. Morgan Chase acquired Bank One in 2004. Immediately prior to joining Delta, he was Vice Chairman of a large Chicago utility for 2 years.

Even today, some must regard Mullin well since he is on the Board of two large companies – Johnson & Johnson and BellSouth, number 30 and number 87 respectively on the 2004 *Fortune* 500 list.

However, it is difficult to see how a Board could consider his management record strong enough to qualify him to lead a major corporation like Delta forward in the increasingly competitive airline industry.

One year after he came to Delta, the Cincinnati Post newspaper said, "Mullin's appointment looked odd" and "Leo Mullin cuts an unlikely figure as an airline boss." It further noted he had never had a job as a chief executive.

An experienced search consultant has said Mullin was the "wrong guy", had "poor judgment", "no instincts for leadership" and "damaged the company." "He had financial acumen. However, he had never demonstrated his leadership capacity; his judgment had never been tested in leadership roles where he had the final answer. So the hiring authorities need to be held accountable."

WHERE WAS THE BOARD?

Mullin's best friend was Ron Allen

Experience has shown that, in general, a new leader has about a six months honeymoon period when they assume the position. The leader's behavior and accomplishments during those six months significantly affect their probability of future success.

Mullin had it luckier. During his first several years on the job, Mullin enjoyed the halo effect anyone replacing Allen would have enjoyed.

Mullin also benefited from the boom economy in the late 1990's.

Most of all, Mullin was quite fortunate to have inherited a company with a strong heritage, knowledgeable employees and a solid senior management team.

In general, employees and executives were glad to have a new leader, particularly one that they thought offered great promise to restore Delta to its rightful position.

Delta people wanted someone who would lead the way to restore it to its former position of superior customer service and profitability and rekindle the spirit of the "Delta family."

They hoped and thought that Mullin would be that leader, but they were unfortunately very wrong.

Out-of-body Experience

Mullin starts off on right foot

Mullin either did his homework or got some good advice. He started on what appeared to be the right foot.

He followed the Delta tradition of CEOs visiting with the front line troops.

For example, the story of his visit with the mechanics in Technical Operations center at around 2 a.m. traveled far and wide.

He made a favorable impression as a nice, polished and articulate executive.

On the surface, Mullin appeared to be a CEO for Delta that was straight out of central casting.

Mullin's true colors start showing early

Upon his arrival at Delta, Mullin asked employees to share with him any ideas they had to make the company better.

I have a copy of a very thoughtful, businesslike letter from a knowledgeable employee responding to Mullin's request.

The employee based the letter on documented facts and experiences.

It made sound strategic suggestions regarding teamwork, quality and performance management. It also addressed significant process issues and concerns.

An employee who loved the company and welcomed Mullin to it wrote the letter from the heart.

Mullin did not consider the effort important enough even to acknowledge it. Of course, Mullin never addressed the substance of the letter.

This is in direct contrast to Mr. Woolman's approach discussed earlier in the book.

Favorable results on 1998 Employee Survey

The results of the 1998 Survey of Delta Personnel showed a dramatic improvement in employee perceptions when compared to the 1996 Survey mentioned above.

These results corroborate both the problem with Allen at the end of his tenure, which would have given any new CEO the benefit of the doubt from employees initially, and the favorable perceptions from Mullin's initial public approach.

- For the question about the company taking an interest in Delta people, unfavorable ratings dropped from 44% to 22%.

- On the respect and dignity treatment question unfavorable responses dropped to 19% from 39%.

- Unfavorable responses to the question about the overall job done by senior management as a group dropped to 14% from 39%.

- Most other responses in the 1998 Survey compared favorably to the 1996 Survey.

- However, these often dramatic changes could not mask the fact that much more work needed to be done by Mullin to repair the problems he inherited.

- The leadership-rating question in the 1996 survey was unfortunately removed in 1998.

Mullin's prescriptions make patient sick

From this point forward, Mullin seems to have made one bad decision after another.

He made senior leadership decisions that compounded earlier bad decisions.

As he added non-Delta people to his senior team, the disconnect with employees and their lack of confidence in management grew.

Like a doctor continuing to prescribe additional drugs to a sick patient, Mullin seemed to add executives without adequate regard for their side effects on the patient or for their interaction with each other.

Internal problems overshadow external

External events, notably Delta's 5th 9/11 on 9/11/2001, certainly affected Delta's performance in the years between 2001 and 2004, when the Board replaced Mullin as CEO.

However, nearly every interviewee laid the main problems at Mullin's feet (and the Board's), particularly the *Executive Compensation Fiasco*, discussed in detail below.

By the time of the terrorist attack on 9/11/2001 the seeds of Mullin's problems with employees and Delta's financial stability had already been sown.

Mullin and his team blamed the fallout from the terrorist attack on Delta's subsequent dismal financial performance.

In fact, the decline in the company's financial performance began prior to 9/11/2001.

Delta had already begun to feel the effects of the financial decisions made by Mullin and his team. The legacy of those decisions made it far more difficult for Delta to respond effectively to the business effects of the terrorist attacks.

The company lost money in the March quarter of 2001. This was the first quarterly loss in seven years.

The last quarterly loss was under Ron Allen in the mid-1990's prior to the Leadership 7.5 initiative.

Mullin's initial steps

Mullin addressed important issues like strategic planning, information technology, financial planning/budgeting and human resources.

To assist him initially, Mullin relied on key members of Allen's Executive Council: Maurice Worth, who had been interim CEO and then later became Mullin's first COO; Bob Coggin, marketing head; Harry Alger, head of flight operations. Mullin quickly replaced former Western CFO Tom Roeck, Delta's CFO from 1987 until 1997.

All of these executives demonstrated a love for Delta and a team attitude by supporting Mullin effectively during his introductory period as Delta's CEO.

They also demonstrated an ability to perform under less than effective leadership in Allen and questionable leadership under Mullin.

It is unfortunate for the company they never had the opportunity after 1987 to serve in senior positions under a CEO who was a true leader.

Mullin's new team begins Delta's fall

It gradually became apparent that Mullin intended to build his team, with the lone exception of Vicki Escarra, entirely from non-Delta people.

He brought in executives from well-known organizations like GE, Arthur Andersen, Frito-Lay and Coke.

However, unfortunately for Delta, one of the few new senior executives familiar with the airline industry was Fred Reid. Mullin hired Reid, formerly COO of Lufthansa, as Chief Marketing Officer and later promoted him to Chief Operating Officer.

Smart, arrogant newcomers with contempt for "Delta family" and culture

A common trait of these new executives was their high intelligence, which they readily displayed at every opportunity.

Most knew little or nothing about the airline business. However, all seemed to understand how to effectively run the numbers to 'prove' their case to each other, Mullin or the Board.

Another common trait was their arrogance with a corollary disdain for Delta history, culture and people. Mullin himself had these traits and clearly seems to have searched for people who shared them.

According to an interviewee who worked closely with him, Mullin made it obvious he thought that Delta's culture is a business 'dinosaur' and so are Delta's people.

Unlike the historical amnesia of Allen, under Mullin the mantra became history was irrelevant.

By discounting or shutting out the input of experienced Delta executives, middle managers and front line employees, Mullin's new team acted as if the world at Delta began when they arrived there.

The few new executives who wisely tried to counsel blending the new ideas into the existing culture did not last.

Thinly veiling his disdain for Delta's heritage, the front cover and Mullin's shareholder letter in the 2001 annual report quoted George Bernard Shaw, "We are made wise not by the recollection of our past, but by the responsibility for our future."

In retrospect, Mullin and his team could have used a lot of the wisdom from Delta's successful past. Had they done so, Delta would arguably not be in the shape it is today.

In that same report, Mullin said, "Our actions throughout 2001 reflected Delta's...dedication to a strong partnership with Delta's people." Soon after the publication of this report, Mullin's actions in the *Executive Compensation Fiasco* demonstrated that, in fact, there was no such partnership in his and his team's mind.

Arrogant attitudes produce arrogant behavior

This new team perceived that Delta's success for 68 years prior to their arrival had been merely a matter of luck, geography and the weak competition from Eastern in its last years.

One member of that team said Delta, in the airline industry, was "regarded as the bumpkin joke in the industry," that the company had always "messed up in reacting to industry situations" and "Delta made money [previously] in spite of itself."

With that preconceived notion, it is understandable but not excusable why these new people would think they were coming into Delta as its saviors instead as its new stewards.

The foundation of the major mistakes made by the Mullin team – mistakes which were instrumental in bringing a fine company to its knees – were the result of this self-perceived intellectual superiority, arrogance and refusal to give credence to important information or opinions if these came from an "old Delta" person.

They created their own game of Monopoly® with brand new rules made out of whole cloth; then demanded that tens of thousands of people blindly follow them without question.

Common sense and people skills scarce

While they may have had mental intelligence, Mullin and his team sorely lacked an understanding of how to relate to people and communicate with them effectively.

As a direct result of this lack of common sense and people skills (what some self-styled gurus now call "emotional intelligence"), the team was able to rule but they never really were able to lead.

Delta people obeyed to keep their job, but they became convinced that the Mullin team never really cared about Delta employees, customers or the company. The *Executive Compensation Fiasco* confirmed their suspicion.

Watch what I say, not what I do

Yet Mullin up to the end – some would say hypocritically because of his and his team's obvious disdain for the values that built the airline– continued to inject quotes from Delta founder C.E. Woolman in his verbal and written remarks.

The 2003 – Mullin's last year as CEO - annual report, celebrated Delta's 75th anniversary. It featured a photograph of Mr.Woolman in front of a crop duster, Delta's first plane.

At the same time, Mullin led a team that operated from a perspective that most interviewees think devalued all that Mr. Woolman believed and bequeathed to those who followed him. The walk did not match the talk.

Revolving door for Mullin CFO's

Mullin went through 5 CFO's in 6 ½ years as Delta CEO.

I believe this lack of continuity contributed greatly to Delta's financial demise under Mullin. It contrasts directly with the 30 years CFO Robert Oppenlander of continuity in sound financial decision making under him.

Mullin quickly replaced Tom Roeck who he inherited from Ron Allen.

Warren Jenson followed for 16 months. Jenson's high-handed behavior was typical of Mullin's crowd.

For example, he once created an embarrassing public firestorm of controversy for Delta and ill will with Delta employees and passengers.

Out-of-body Experience

To the amazement and consternation of the "Delta family," Jenson's secretary forced a gate agent to move seated first-class passengers to coach so three of Jenson's kids, all flying free, could fly first class and their friend, flying on a discounted coach ticket could get a first class upgrade. This incident not only offended the four inconvenienced passengers but also delayed the departure of the flight by 24 minutes.

Had Mr. Woolman been alive, he would have summarily dismissed Jenson and had him escorted off Delta property. Instead, Mullin had a private meeting with Jenson. The outcome of that meeting was a slap on Jenson's wrist. Mullin allowed him to get off the hook by reimbursing Delta for the $1,000 in vouchers given the bumped passengers and writing a mea culpa memorandum to Delta employees. Adding insult to injury, the memorandum said, "This has been a very difficult week for me and my family." He and his family also lost their free flight privileges for six months; Jenson had left for Amazon.com before that time expired.

Jenson's successor was Ed Bastian, a long time Delta employee (who later left Delta and was recently rehired by current CEO Gerald Grinstein).

Then in September 1999, Mullin promoted Ed West, a 33 year old employed by Delta for 5 years. West remained as CFO for less than a year.

Mullin's last CFO was Michelle Burns, a former tax partner in the Atlanta office of Arthur Andersen public accounting firm, now defunct as a result of the Enron scandal in their Houston office. (Coincidentally, *Consultant X* gets credit for being the prime architect for Enron of the energy trading strategy that led to Enron's implosion.)

She joined Delta in 1999 as VP/Corporate Taxes; in January 2000, she received a promotion to Senior VP/Finance and Treasurer; in August 2000, Mullin made her CFO, the position she held until a few months after Gerald Grinstein became CEO in January 2004.

Burns was instrumental in the *Executive Compensation Fiasco* that eventually ended the reign of Mullin and his team and in the financial decisions that have contributed to Delta's disastrous condition now.

Questions about Delta's pension plan investments

A reliable source told me that Delta, under Mullin and Burns, had taken what many would consider excessive risks with Delta's pension plan investments. Specifically, many of the plan's assets allegedly were moved from safer, lower yielding investments to risky, higher yielding ones.

The purpose of this move was to inflate artificially the earnings of the company. Accounting rules allow a company to include the performance of its employee pension plans in its overall financial results.

I was unable to assess directly the accuracy of this allegation. However, if it is true, then Delta employees may have been harmed even more than they now know.

For example, if these high-risk investments have gone down considerably in value, that would have the effect of increasing the pension plan underfunding situation that Delta, its retirees and employees now face.

Those now seeking redress for wrongs done to Delta's pension plan should assess this situation. As I understand Federal regulations, any Delta employee or retiree has the right to request the report Delta must periodically file that details the investments of the company's pension plan.

Interviewees for this book were particularly incensed when asked their reaction to this possible use of Delta pension funds.

One CEO, who was formerly a CFO, said, "This is trying to get a quick win with other people's money. They would have violated their fiduciary responsibility."

Another CEO said, "You are gambling with employees' future and not taking a long view of the corporation's future. The mentality seems to be the same as the executive pension decision. This is looking out for the higher echelons at the expense of the employees."

WHERE WAS THE BOARD?

Mullin abdicates Delta for Washington

After 9/11/2001, Mullin quickly assumed the position as spokesperson for the industry in Washington to ask for financial help for airlines to make up for some of their losses following the attacks.

For all practical purposes, he turned over running Delta to his subordinates and focused his attention on a government bailout.

With Reid as Chief Operating Officer, the Delta management team was supposed to function effectively while Mullin was off pleading for money from the politicians.

However, those familiar with Reid's management style say he came to the office only sporadically, choosing to work from home. In addition, it was apparently difficult to schedule a meeting with him, since he often would be in California at his ranch.

Reaction to Mullin's Washington focus

Interviewees, particularly Delta employees and retirees, showed mixed feelings about Mullin's efforts in Washington.

Initially these efforts were perceived as a good thing for the industry and for Delta. However, as time passed people began to ask, "Who is minding the store?" at Delta.

One very senior executive, retired from a large company and now lead Board member of another successful company, said "Delta was so far in the tank, for him [Mullin] to be out there as industry spokesman didn't make sense." He went further to say, "He [Mullin] was so focused on these activities [Washington] nobody was paying attention to the details of running the airline. It took a back seat to what might have appeared more glamorous."

More than a few employees and others perceive that Mullin's ultimate goal had been a Washington appointment for a long time and his visible Washington presence was more to cement his future as a government appointee than to help the airline industry and Delta.

It could have been an urban legend, but some perceived Mullin thought he would be the likely nominee (and a very willing one) for Transportation Secretary had Senator Gore won the 2000 presidential election.

Based on this, it appeared to them that Mullin's unstated purpose for his Washington focus after

9/11/2001 was to set the stage for a subsequent high-level appointment with the Federal government.

Supporting the theory that Mullin may have wanted a government appointment is the fact that he spent about 8 years in the Washington office of *Consultant X* earlier in his career.

Beginning of the end for Mullin team and Delta going into the financial tank

The beginning of the end for Mullin and his entire executive team – and a major catalyst in Delta's financial misfortunes ever since – was late 2001 and early 2002.

Some time shortly after 9/11/2001, while Mullin was in Washington pleading his case before Congress, back home some of his direct reports were concocting an executive compensation scheme to protect themselves financially, particularly their pensions.

Mullin and the Delta Board kept this scheme secret for a year between January 2002 and early 2003.

Once the scheme was made public through a mandatory Delta financial filing, it received immediate, widespread news coverage in Atlanta, around the country and around the world.

The scheme seriously damaged the company and ultimately led to Mullin's resignation as CEO effective January 1, 2004. Within a few months after that, all of his direct reports had left the company.

Executive Compensation Fiasco

The Delta Board's Personnel & Compensation Committee (consisting of Mr. Budd, chairperson, along with Messrs. Fisher, Goode and Grinstein) approved the *Executive Compensation Fiasco* in January 2002.

A proposal to protect management pensions and their incomes became a topic of intense discussion in the executive ranks in late 2001.

Various people reportedly pushed back on the idea along the way out of concern over how employees would perceive it, particularly since all employees other than the 35 (33 publicly documented names plus 2 others not documented) were then being told their pension benefits were going to be cut.

Those possibly included long-time Delta family member Vicki Escarra, Executive Vice President/Marketing and Revenue Management; another long-time Delta family member, Robert Harkey, Executive Vice President/Chief Counsel. One interviewee also mentioned Robert Colman, Executive Vice President/Human Resources, who had come in from GE, although another strenuously doubted that he would have taken that position.

It must have been hard for any executive to question the wisdom of the proposal since it would, if implemented, amount to hundreds of thousands or millions of dollars in each of their pockets, thus cementing their financial future at a very high level.

Ultimately, Mullin agreed with the proposal and allowed it to go to the Board's Personnel & Compensation Committee for their approval.

I was unable to verify directly the Committee's discussion about the proposal because Delta declined my request for access to its minutes.

One source indicated that Grinstein, and perhaps others, questioned how employees might react to the program, once it became public.

This would have been a logical concern since the company was shifting employees from a defined benefit pension plan to a much less valuable defined contribution pension plan.

At the same time employee pensions were being cut, the proposal called for executive pensions being secured and increased. These executives were being given the opportunity to receive extra bonuses as well.

Delta Board sweetens executives' pie

The basics of the *Executive Compensation Fiasco* approved by the Personnel & Compensation Committee were:

- *Special Retention Program* – A contingent cash retention award tied to the executive's base salary. This ranged from 125% to 300% of the executive's base salary. The award was subject to the executive remaining with Delta through 2003 to earn 33%; then remaining with the company through 2004 to receive the remaining 67%. There was a provision that the second payment could be made in early 2004 if Delta's EBITDAR Margin for the two-year period ending 12/31/2003 was at or above the comparable figure for an airline peer group.

- *Pension Trusts* – The Internal Revenue Service code limits the benefits that can be paid from a qualified retirement plan like the one that covered all Delta employees, including executives. To pay executives pensions above the maximum IRS allowed limits, the company had set up an unfunded, non-qualified retirement plan. Qualified plans are protected to a limited degree by the Pension Benefit Guaranty Corporation, which can pay a reduced percentage of benefits the retiree would have gotten had their employer not gone into bankruptcy; non-qualified plans have no such limited protection. To secure their extra pension benefits the executives formulated and the Board approved funding pension trusts for 33 top people to address the "significant concern for retention of management personnel." I understand two more were added later, but have been unable to document that. The company contributed $ 25.5 million to these trusts in 2002 to secure 60% of the value of these executives' pension benefits and also paid the taxes due from the executives for these contributions; The balance was scheduled to be paid in 2003 and 2004 "to further enhance the retention value of this program" according to the 2003 Delta proxy statement.

Year long Executive Compensation Fiasco cover-up

Although the Board approved the above special executive perquisites in January 2002, they were kept secret from employees, stockholders, analysts and the press until a year later, when they were divulged in one of Delta's mandatory filings with the Federal government.

One interviewee said the 'party line' rationale for keeping these lavish executive perquisites secret at the time was that management did not want to upset the employees who were struggling to deal with the post 9/11 situation.

Neither management nor the Board demonstrated adequate appreciation for the deep and permanent mistrust of the management team this planned secrecy would create.

Based on my interviews and my knowledge of Delta, I believe that an announcement of the perquisites immediately after the Board granted them would have been poorly received. I doubt that employees would have bought into the "retention" argument any more in January 2002 than they did in early 2003.

However, an immediate disclosure and explanation would have removed the perception that management may have engaged in a planned deception.

The perception created with employees by timely disclosure would have been one of unfair treatment but not deception as well.

Reid interview when cover-up began

Delta President and Chief Operating Officer Fred Reid was interviewed by "HR Atlanta" newspaper at the time the *Executive Compensation Fiasco* was approved.

In their February 2002 issue the interview ran under a headline of 'Flying Delta Air Lines Through the 9/11 Storm'.

Reid was asked what had been learned about employee relations at Delta as a result of 9/11.

Reid responded, "Communicate, communicate, communicate with the employees. But this means more than sending out memos and e-mails. The management team has to be widely visible and accessible, (This may sound familiar since it was Mr. Woolman's philosophy and the way Delta was run for 68 years before the Mullin people took over. It seems 9/11 provided Reid and his fellow executives with an epiphany.) **has to disclose as much information as possible about what they know and,** equally important, what they don't know, **and has to be truthful in all they say**." The executive perquisites granted immediately before this article ran apparently did not pass management's threshold for disclosure and truthfulness.

Delta had a post 9/11 Airline Action Plan. A folding wallet size mini-brochure, reportedly sponsored by Reid, provided employees with the key strategies in that plan.

One of those strategies was 'Care' stating 'We care for our customers, our company and each other. We support an inclusive culture where people communicate openly and are recognized for their contributions. Together, we make Delta a great place to work'.

It is hard to justify hiding the *Executive Compensation Fiasco* for a year in light of this strategy and the others in the plan.

The leadership lesson here is that employees and customers watch what leaders do, not what they say. If you don't mean it, don't say it

Everyone in "Delta family" asked to suffer except executives

During the year of secrecy regarding the *Executive Compensation Fiasco* employee pensions were changed from Delta's longstanding defined benefit plan (the company commits to a specific pension payment) to a far less valuable defined contribution (401k type) plan.

Exacerbating the problem for Mullin and the Board was they implemented the multi-million dollar *Executive Compensation Fiasco* in a year when Delta lost $1.3 *billion*. This was on top of the $1.6 *billion* loss in 2001. Therefore, stockholders were clearly suffering.

Also during the year of secrecy, management was negotiating with the pilots' union ALPA (Air Line Pilots Association) to get post 9/11 relief from the expensive contract Mullin had provided them several months earlier. (One Delta pilot told me he was surprised at the contract when it was announced and recalled thinking, "Mullin gave away the store.") This contract made Delta pilots the most highly paid in the industry and Mullin bragged about that at the time. After 9/11, those pilot costs became a significant impediment to the company's financial health.

Job cuts had already begun in 2001 when 7,653 Delta people lost their jobs. During 2002 Delta also was cutting jobs, ending the year with 1,200 fewer employees than at the end of 2001. They cut an additional 4,500 employees in 2003. Overall, 13,353 employees – or 15.9% of the 83,952 Delta people at the beginning - were cut during the three-year period between 1/1/2001 and 12/31/2003.

This contrasts dramatically to the security and highly favorable compensation provided Delta executives during the same period. For example the company paid 60 of the top executives $17.3 million in cash performance bonuses in 2002.

The "Alice in Wonderland" rationale for executives receiving large bonuses was the creative compensation scheme to tie bonuses to cash instead of profits since Delta was losing billions. One interviewee, the CEO of the U.S. subsidiary of a global company and former CFO, said about the concept of tying bonuses to cash (after laughing out loud when he heard the idea), "All the executives had to do [to earn their cash-based bonuses] was sell company assets, lease them back and create a windfall."

The bottom line of these bonuses based on cash instead of profits is they encouraged Mullin and his crowd to mortgage Delta, which they did exceedingly well, as the financial statements and current condition now reflect. WHERE WAS THE BOARD?

One interviewee, a former CFO and CEO who built a successful national company, said of the entire *Executive Compensation Fiasco*, "It is incomprehensible that people are so arrogant that they would say you have to guarantee me so many dollars to stay."

He went further to say, "WHERE IS THE BOARD? If they (the Board) were being held hostage, tell them (the executives) to get the h--- out. A Board is guilty of negligence for not firing the people when they bring those kinds of arguments forth." Delta would not be in its weakened condition today had the Board done so.

Secrecy veil lifted from Executive Compensation Fiasco

The annual proxy statement required by the U.S. Securities and Exchange Commission to be filed by all publicly held companies was filed by Delta in January 2003.

Even then, there was no press announcement or disclosure to employees.

Once they saw the SEC filing, a group of retired Delta executives worked behind the scenes to ask management to request their non-qualified pensions be given the same protection as the active executives. Delta rebuffed this request.

When the retirees subsequently saw the FY 2002 financial results, showing a second straight year of a $1.25 billion loss, they decided to withdraw their request and to ask the company to rescind the special perquisites that had been granted.

Once the veil of secrecy was removed any chance of pilot concessions vanished, as common sense would predict, although the union formally denied any link between executive compensation and that of the pilot group.

Both sides went through the motions sporadically during 2003 with little substantive progress. The union sat down at the bargaining table for serious discussions only after Mullin was gone as CEO and Gerald Grinstein had worked very hard to build trust among employees and to communicate the message of Delta's financial reality directly to pilots and their families.

Executive retention scheme doesn't retain

The facts underscore the failure of the *Executive Compensation Fiasco* to achieve the stated goal of retaining a close-knit management team during tough times for the company.

This failure also underscores the perception of many that the real purpose was simply "another case of corporate greed" as one CEO interviewee said.

- Of the 33 publicly known participants in the pension trust part of the plan, only 9 remain with the company. Barely 1 out of 4 of the group was 'retained' by Delta.

- The initially secret first payments to the trusts in early 2002 totaled $25.5 million to cover the pension payment and taxes for 60% of the total overall value of the trusts. The balance was to be funded in the second and third years to insure executive retention.

- Mullin and his top four officers – Reid, Escarra, Colman and Burns – collectively received 55.5% of the total 2002 pensions trust payments. They are all gone from the company.

- The 24 people who have left the company to date accounted for 94.02% of the total 2002 pension trust payments.

- There were 9 lawyers among the 33 executives who received the trusts or more than 25% of the total group. Delta demonstrated that retaining their legal team seemed an important part of managing the company during tough times.

- The lawyers who have left the company accounted for 86.7% of the $4.6 million in 2002 pension trust payments to those in the legal department.

Mullin loses ability to lead but Board allows him to hang on for months

Once the *Executive Compensation Fiasco* became public, Mullin and his team immediately lost their ability to lead and any moral authority they may have been able to exercise up to that time.

It would have been better for Delta had either the Board or Mullin immediately acknowledged the inevitable – that Mullin had to go.

Instead, the Board allowed him to remain as CEO for another 10 months and Chairman for another 14 months. During this period, Mullin was both a lame duck and a constant reminder that management and Delta employees were no longer on the same team.

Mullin, because of his preeminent role in asking for Congressional handouts for the airline industry, continually reinforced Washington's perception of executive greed, decreasing the willingness to help the industry as a result. That reluctance continues even today.

None of the interviewees believes that the Mullin team actions reflected the 'partnership' in his written and verbal statements.

There is an applicable Southern expression, "That dog don't hunt," meaning something is not what someone is telling you it is. In brief, it is not credible.

The lawyer for the retired executives who challenged Mullin on the pension trusts was quoted in the

Atlanta Journal-Constitution, "If Leo Mullin were the captain of the Titanic, he would be the first person in the lifeboat."

Due to their strong influence over Mullin and their key role in the *Executive Compensation Fiasco*, one interviewee had a different view. They said, "No. [CFO] Michelle [Burns] and [President/COO] Fred [Reid] would be first [in the lifeboat]. They would tell Leo to follow them."

An indication of Mullin's malleability is allowing his spouse to take over his office. A knowledgeable interviewee told me that the "Mahogany Row" support staff watched in amazement as Mrs. Mullin would assume control of his mail, go through it and then tell him what he needed to do to run Delta.

Mullin allowed to hang on, Carty out immediately

Rick McKay / Cox Newspapers

Delta CEO Mullin (left) and American CEO Carty testifying before the U.S. House Aviation Subcommittee in September 2002 asking for more Federal money for airlines. They had each received bankruptcy-proof multi-million dollar pension trust payments earlier in 2002, shortly after 9/11/2001. Several months after their Congressional testimony, the trust payments first became public knowledge. Carty was terminated within a month of public disclosure. The Delta Board allowed Mullin to stay as CEO after public disclosure in early 2003 until his resignation as CEO effective 12/31/ 2003 and eventual departure from the company in April 2004.

This is in contrast to Donald Carty, former CEO at American Airlines, who pulled a similar pension fiasco. Carty resigned under fire with no severance package about a month after his fiasco became public.

Like Mullin he hid the existence of fat "retention" bonuses for top executives and the $41 million pension trust set up so he and the other executives would get their pensions even if the company filed for bankruptcy.

These executive perquisites were kept secret until immediately after American employees had been persuaded by Carty to accept $1.8 billion in pay cuts. Carty walked out the door with a $1 million annual pension.

Both Carty and Mullin appeared before the U.S. Congress during 2002 [see photo on previous page] to passionately appeal for financial aid to airlines to compensate for their post-9/11 financial difficulties.

While they were testifying both men were already protected by multi-million dollar pension trust packages protecting them no matter what happened to their respective airline. Once that became public, the industry lost complete credibility in Washington and still has credibility problems to this day.

This is evidenced by the lukewarm Congressional response, as of this writing, to the industry's request (including Delta) to have more time to make up for pension plan underfunding.

Once the Delta fiasco become public, Senator John McCain said if he saw Leo Mullin among executives visiting lawmakers on Capitol Hill, he would tell him "You ought to be ashamed of yourself."

Mullin's long shadow continues to harm Delta.

WHERE WAS THE BOARD?

Ineffective damage control and non-apology apologies

From the moment the Delta *Executive Compensation Fiasco* became public knowledge, Mullin and his team permanently lost their ability to lead.

Nothing he could say would ever have regained his credibility as the CEO with employees, the government, customers or the business community.

Mullin and the Board exacerbated the situation by feeble, half-hearted damage control attempts. For example, reducing his and COO Fred Reid's salaries and his bonus and retention payments for 2003 was merely a band-aid on terminal cancer.

His April 2003 employee memo announcing this decision stated, "In the current circumstances, the steps I am taking feel right to me." This halfhearted effort smacks of "Now that you caught me, I am doing the least I can do to try to end the flap." It didn't work.

Mullin faces the inevitable and is allowed to resign

In the fall of 2003, Mullin had unsuccessfully spent months trying to quench the flames resulting from the *Executive Compensation Fiasco*, but instead continued to fan them by his presence.

Delta quietly conducted telephone interviews with some employees at their homes over a weekend. Reportedly, these interviews were to determine the level of confidence employees had in management.

Unlike the results of the favorable 1998 Employee Survey, the results of these telephone interviews were never made public. Based on the continuing high level of employee dissatisfaction prior to the interviews, it seems likely that they were unfavorable, most likely highly unfavorable.

Shortly after the interviews were completed, Mullin announced his retirement.

Grinstein's philosophical 'apology'

Grinstein, in a memo to employees on 12/24/2003 immediately before he was to become CEO on 1/1/2004, did announce cuts in the executive pay program to 'clear the air'.

In a classic understatement he said, "An executive compensation package that includes normal elements such as earned incentive pay (sometimes called 'bonuses') can seem inappropriate when the company is losing money and other employees are making sacrifices."

To his credit, one of the principles Grinstein laid down to guide future executive compensation decisions was, "When sacrifice is required, it should be shared by all employee groups." Of course, this principle of shared sacrifice is one of the basic precepts that guided the Delta family from its founding up to the time Mullin became CEO.

Many Delta family members have expressed their gratitude that it is now guiding the family again. Grinstein also took a salary of $500,000 − far less than Mullin and that of most other CEO's of large companies − with no other executive perquisites other than a generous relocation allowance. This decision also sent a message to the troops that a new day may have dawned at Delta.

However, no one – Mullin, Grinstein or anyone on the Board - has ever fully acknowledged they made a terrible mistake with the *Executive Compensation Fiasco*– one that has damaged the company severely, perhaps irreparably. Instead, Mullin made statements apologizing for the flap that the decision created, never apologizing for the decision itself. Grinstein allowed him to do that.

Financial results document destruction to Delta by the Mullin team

The financial and operating results of Mullin and his team from 6/30/1997 (the FY ended on 6/30 until 2000 when the FY end was changed to a calendar year) until his departure as CEO on 12/31/2003 show the serious financial damage done to Delta during that time.

Mullin did not step down as Chairman until late spring, 2004 and many of the decisions made under his tenure as CEO impacted the 2004 financial results.

Therefore, the 2004 results comparable to the 6/30/1997 – 12/31/2003 results are also shown below.

While Allen seriously damaged the Delta culture and harmed employee loyalty greatly, when he left Delta on 6/30/1997, it had just completed the best year financially in the history of the company.

Financially, Mullin took over a solid company and left Delta in terrible shape as the statistics below demonstrate.

Like the undeserving kids getting an inheritance from a rich uncle, Mullin and his team took over an airline rich in cash, assets and employee loyalty, then nearly squandered it all (except for what they protected to put in their pockets). The Delta Board clearly provided no meaningful parental restraints during the squandering.

Although Mullin was replaced as CEO on January 1, 2004, statistics for the latter year are also shown to reflect the fact that the momentum in place when Mullin left was a key determinant in 2004 results.

Long-term debt and capital leases

- Increased $9.7 billion or 539% – from $1.8 billion to $11.5 billion
- Total for 2004 increased to $13.0 billion

Shareholders' Equity

- Declined $3.7 billion – from $3.0 billion to -$.7 billion
- Further dramatic decline in 2004 to -$5.8 billion

Net Profit/Loss

- Went from an $845 million profit in 1997 to a loss of $773 million in 2003
- This does not reflect the 2004 loss of $5.2 billion, which is largely attributable to the Mullin legacy (he remained as Chairman until spring 2004 although he resigned as CEO on 12/31/2003) and the significant restructuring costs his successor Gerald Grinstein's team had to incur.

On *three key financial metrics* in the airline industry, all were in worse shape when Mullin left:

Operating revenue/available seat mile (ASM) – ASM is a measure of capacity

- Increased slightly by 1.6% from $9.94 to $10.10
- Declined slightly to $9.89 in 2004

Operating cost/available seat mile (CASM) – unit cost

- Increased a significant 20.9% from $8.82 to $10.66
- Dramatic increase to $12.07 in 2004

Spread between operating revenue/ASM and operating cost/ASM

- Positive spread of $1.12 in 1997
- Negative spread in 2003 of - $.56/ASM, an indication that the airline could not make money with the cost and revenue structure put in place by Mullin.
- Negative spread increased in 2004 to $2.18, meaning it *cost* Delta $2.18 for every ASM flown

Operating results were equally unfavorable:

Passenger load factor (the % of total seats available filled with paying passengers determined by dividing Revenue Passenger Miles – RPM – by ASM)

- Remained relatively constant moving slightly higher from 71.4% to 73.3%

- Increased to 74.7% under Grinstein in 2004

Breakeven load factor (the % of total seats available that must be filled to begin making a profit)

- Increased from 62.7% to 77.8% - a significant 24.1% jump – which was higher than the actual load factor achieved

- Continued to escalate in 2004 rising to 92.6%

Full-time employees (FTE)

- Increased to 70,600 from 63,441

- This 11.3% increase wiped out all the personnel reductions from the Leadership 7.5 initiative in the mid-1990's. FTE's were at 69,555 at the start of that initiative in 1994. ***Therefore, all the pain and suffering of the thousands who had to leave the company and those left behind who had to endure 7.5 was for naught.***

- In fact, Mullin had increased head count to 83,952 by 12/31/2000. He had to cut out almost 14,000 jobs, creating more pain and disruption, in order to get to the still inflated head count of 70,600 on 12/31/2003.

- When the current CEO Gerald Grinstein took over in January 2004, he was in the position where Delta people again were subjected to another prolonged round of job reductions, which is still underway, to attempt survival.

- Grinstein eliminated 1,450 in 2004; his goal is to eliminate an additional 6,000 jobs by the end of 2005.

- If the latter goal is achieved it is ironic that the Delta head count will then be back almost exactly where it was when Mullin took over in 1997 from Allen.

Total number of aircraft in the fleet

- Increased over 50% from 553 to 833. This helps explain the dramatic increase in long-term debt discussed above.

- Since there were only modest increases during Mullin's 6 ½ year period in the need for these aircraft it becomes clearer how the company was led to the shape in which the Mullin team left it.

- Annual revenue passengers increased only 3.3%; ASM's increased only 2.0%; revenue passenger miles increased only 4.7%.

- There were 845 aircraft in the fleet at the end of 2004, with the increase primarily attributable to the addition of regional jets.

Mullin's amazing statements at the end

The Board allowed Mullin to save face by 'retiring' as CEO in late 2003 while remaining as Board Chairman until mid- 2004.

Despite all the damage done to Delta under Mullin, Board member and now CEO Gerald Grinstein, who had the primary responsibility for hiring Mullin, sang Mullin's praises up to and including when Mullin left the company.

USA Today interviewed Mullin in late 2003 about his impending retirement. In the interview, one month before the close of Delta's 2003 fiscal year when it lost almost $800 million following a loss of about $1.25 billion in 2002, Mullin said, "The company is doing OK financially."

If losing $2.0 billion in two years is doing OK financially, one can only speculate what Mullin would consider doing poorly.

In that same interview, Mullin also said he had been planning retirement for more than a year. That focus on his personal needs, along with his focus on industry-wide needs, supports the contention that Delta was without a pilot at the stick of the company during his tenure.

It is also difficult to reconcile Mullin's statement in late 2003 with the stated reason – "executive retention" – for the perquisites in the *Executive Compensation Fiasco* granted in early 2002.

It would appear that Mullin started planning retirement immediately after the perquisites were granted or that he had already been planning retirement before they were granted. Either way it is difficult to see how the executive retention argument accurately and truthfully represented the facts.

As one interviewee, a highly regarded, retired CEO, has often said to me, "Things ultimately speak on their own merits."

If, in fact, Mullin had been "discussing retirement for over a year", then WHERE WAS THE BOARD? If Mullin mentally had one foot out the door, why would the Board allow someone to remain as CEO of a company facing tough sledding like Delta, much less give him lucrative "retention" incentives that were worth millions to him immediately?

Mullin and team now take up first class space from paying passengers on Delta

A front line Delta employee told me, "It is unconscionable that Leo Mullin can fly (Delta) positive space first class for the rest of his life."

This privilege enables Mullin to reserve and fly free in a first class seat that otherwise could be sold to a paying passenger on Delta, which needs all the revenue it can get, largely because of the terrible financial shape in which he left it.

Recently a friend who flies Delta frequently on business was on standby for a first class upgrade. Instead, Mullin decided to take that flight and he got the last first class seat. My friend was bumped back to coach. Delta gave priority to the man who may have destroyed the company over a valuable customer.

Mullin gets credit for his gall. Many hope that as Delta looks at contracts they must break during bankruptcy, they put Mullin's flight privileges at the top of the list.

In addition, the others on Mullin's executive team who left the company enjoy the same privilege of flying positive space first class free for life, also bumping paying passengers while being served by Delta employees whose jobs, salaries and pensions they decimated.

Mullin leaves behind mess and walks out with millions

Mullin walked out the door with a $16 million retirement package from Delta, a company bleeding financially and which got into that position while he was leading it.

Mullin left a mess for Delta employees to clean up and a difficult struggle for survival.

He now provides advice to Johnson & Johnson and BellSouth as a member of their respective Board of Directors.

7 – Delta's Fight for Survival

Long-time Board member Gerald Grinstein replaced Mullin as CEO on January 1, 2004. Jack Smith, retired Chairman of General Motors, replaced Mullin as Delta's non-executive Board Chairman on July 1, 2004.

Grinstein steps to the plate

With Delta's back against the financial wall, Grinstein took over as Delta's pilot - the first true leader of an airline without one for 16 ½ years.

Allen was a pilot but not a captain; Mullin was not even a pilot at all.

There is wide admiration for Jerry's willingness to step to the plate to lead Delta during what is arguably the toughest time in Delta's history.

Inheriting from Mullin a patient that was on life support, Jerry has worked hard to lead the Delta team to first keep the 'patient' alive, and then move it to the Intensive Care Unit and eventually out of the hospital.

Age 71 when he took over, Grinstein had "made his money," as evidenced by his buying Bill Gates' former home in Seattle and then tearing it down to build another one more to his and his wife Lyn's liking.

He has run two sizable corporations – Western Airlines (part of Delta since 1987) and Burlington Northern Railroad) - and sold or merged both into larger organizations.

Based on his record of accomplishment in other organizations, Grinstein has shown his ability to lead and to make money. He has nothing to prove to anyone.

Grinstein's refreshing approach

Grinstein began treating long-time Delta employees as if they had some sense, a refreshing contrast from Mullin and his crowd.

He treated them like dedicated, experienced professionals, as they deserved to be treated. Involving a broad group of Delta people, he led the development of Delta's Transformation Plan – intended to change the business model to address industry realities in a unique way.

In general, Grinstein communicated directly and effectively about issues of concern to employees and about the direction in which he hoped to lead the company.

Balancing a positive attitude about his intent and hope for a positive future for Delta, he was straightforward about the magnitude of the task. Grinstein never devolved into hyperbole that would have reduced his credibility.

He has been reliably consistent in all his communications about the Transformation Plan. This has reassured employees and others that Delta once again had a leader and plan to succeed.

Once again, Delta people were encouraged to feel justifiable pride in the company they helped build.

Grinstein also treated Delta's heritage and culture with dignity and respect, a dramatic departure from the Mullin era.

He led Delta to address the fundamental strategic issues that the Mullin people either ignored or misdirected.

Most of all, he began to give the "Delta family" hope that Delta might once again be restored to its traditional and rightful place as a highly regarded, profitable airline providing quality service to customers.

Who is Gerald Grinstein?

Unlike Mullin, Grinstein knows the airline business.

His behavior since becoming CEO indicated he "gets it" about Delta's unique history, culture and the values on which the company was built.

He gives the impression of sharing and living similar values. So far he has shown the Delta family that he will walk the talk, something that had been sorely absent for almost 7 years.

Specifically Jerry demonstrates an understanding that the foundation of airline customer service is dedicated employees working together as a team to provide good service. (If that approach sounds familiar, remember that is how Mr. Woolman and Delta employees built a successful airline that was profitable for decades.)

Recognizing the tremendous effort of Delta employees during his first transitional year as CEO and the results they achieved (in spite of the record-breaking losses), Grinstein dedicated 2005, the company's 76th year in business, as the "Year of Delta's Employees."

Grinstein walks the talk by sharing the pain with Delta employees

He seems to understand that Delta people want management to be on the same team with them, sharing the pain as well as any successes.

As a result, he has taken no perquisites (except for relocation expenses of approximately $100,000) and a salary of $500,000, small by standards of CEO's running companies comparable to Delta's size. In September 2004, he even forfeited his salary for the last 3 months of that year. Recently, it reduced to $337,500.

Grinstein took the above voluntary action to show he was sharing the financial pain at the same time he announced actions that would cause pain for employees. These actions included an across the board 10% salary reduction for all non-pilot employees on January 1, 2005; reduction of officers' total compensation of 25% - 45% from 2003 to 2004 on top of an 8% reduction in March 2003; reduction in vacation leave and increase in employees' share of health care costs.

Immediately following the above announcement, after months of protracted negotiations beginning under Mullin, Delta's pilots union agreed to take a 32.5% pay reduction, along with benefit decreases, to help stave off bankruptcy. Annual savings are $1 billion.

As the pilot agreement demonstrates, people have noticed his actions, particularly since they are in such stark contrast to Mullin and his crowd who most interviewees said, in one expression or another, they believe "robbed the company."

Grinstein's work ethic

His work ethic has earned wide respect. In early 2004, shortly after Jerry took over as CEO, he was commuting every weekend back to his home in Seattle. While there, he was working every weekend on Delta business, even calling officers on Sunday to discuss business issues.

Recently he was in Washington testifying before Congress in a morning hearing on airline pension issues. Following that hearing, he flew back to Atlanta for the afternoon. Then he took an overnight flight from Atlanta to Amsterdam for a business meeting there the following day. That is impressive commitment from anyone, particularly a 73-year-old person.

Grinstein sends a frugality message

Executive parking spaces are in clear view of headquarters employees. When Jerry first came to work at Delta, he drove a Chevrolet Impala, sending a clear strong message to employees that he understood the need for frugality by everyone in the company.

This was in direct contrast to the expensive vehicles then being driven by executives on Delta's Mahogany Row, the name employees use to refer to the executives offices at the General Offices or GO (Deltaspeak for headquarters). Jerry now drives one of the hybrid cars, another sign of the need to conserve.

Grinstein honors Delta's traditions

He listened to Delta people regarding the company image, particularly the trademarked 'widget' logo. Delta used this logo for many years prior to Mullin's crowd deciding to "update" it, in a costly, unnecessary exercise. Grinstein brought the 'widget' back.

In another visible sign he embraces the values of Mr. Woolman, Grinstein had the furniture from Mr. Woolman's office brought to his office to replace what Mullin had left. Then Mullin's furniture, including a chair that reportedly cost $18,000, was moved into storage.

Grinstein the person

Jerry is an engaging man, one that most people instantly like and want to get to know when they meet him for the first time. He looks you straight in the eye and listens intently to what is being said to him.

He is a sophisticated lawyer and business person but communicates concepts in a way that people at all levels can understand and to which they can relate.

His wife has impressed a Delta flight attendant who has flown with them as "nice person who is enjoyable to talk to." The Grinsteins are unpretentious people; Delta people appreciate that, particularly after the contrasting behavior exhibited by Mullin and his team.

Perceptions of Grinstein

Many interviewees think Grinstein has made a remarkable effort to lead Delta under extremely difficult circumstances, in spite of the bankruptcy filing.

However, sizable portions of those believe he is dealing with a situation that he played the lead role in creating.

One frontline employee said, "I think he feels guilty for having brought in Leo Mullin."

Grinstein's first 18 months a financial disaster

Delta had $3.3 billion in cumulative net losses with Mullin as CEO during the three years prior to Grinstein taking over.

During 2004, in Grinstein's first year as CEO, Delta lost $5.2 billion, a one-year record in the airline industry. However, arguably this loss is primarily the result of the downward spiral started under Mullin that it took Grinstein a year to slow down.

Although Grinstein has slowed the financial bleeding, the airline lost an additional $1.5 in the first 6 months of 2005.

Combined losses during the past 4 ½ years are $10.0 billion.

Delta's 6th 9/11

After a nearly 20-month struggle to turn Delta around and avoid bankruptcy, the company filed for Chapter 11 bankruptcy protection on September 14, 2005.

This was a sad day for everyone in both the immediate and extended "Delta family" – a day perhaps as sad in its own way as the death of Mr. Woolman almost 40 years before.

Part of the sadness is because of the memory of how successful Delta once was and the resulting pride employees felt about the company and the service they helped provide.

Another part comes from the intense, prolonged struggle by employees to do their part to bring their company back to its former position and then having to face an awful result – one so foreign that few thought it possible even 5 years ago.

The sadness mixes with fear – fear by employees and retirees, their families, stockholders, customers, vendors, taxpayers, governments and all others among the tens of thousands impacted by the bankruptcy.

Foundation for bankruptcy laid long ago

Grinstein's 9/14/05 email to employees informing them of the bankruptcy filing, as well as his call-in line for Delta employees, said:

"So why did we voluntarily decide to restructure through the courts now, when we have worked so hard for so long to recover on our own? Simply put, persistent record-high fuel prices and the aggressive pricing pressures brought on by low-cost carriers (LCCs) intent on beating us outpaced and masked the significant progress we've made with our Transformation Plan [discussed later in this chapter]. Despite everyone's sacrifice and the significant improvements we are making together, unless we took this step we soon would no longer have had enough cash to run our operation, pay our bills and protect our assets."

It is obvious to anyone who even occasionally reads a newspaper or watches television news that the two factors cited by Grinstein – high fuel costs and increasing price competition from low-cost carriers - as prompting the filing are real for every airline, just as they have been for Delta.

It is also true that Delta employees, under Grinstein's leadership, have made remarkable strides in the last 20 months to recover from the awful situation in which Mullin left Delta. (In a note of irony, a TV reporter, who intercepted him scurrying through the Atlanta airport, interviewed Mullin on the evening of the bankruptcy announcement. Mullin, clearly quite uncomfortable at the walking interview, said about Delta, "They are good people. I wish them the best." I doubt those "good people" now losing their jobs, and perhaps pensions, because of Mullin wish him the best.)

Leadership produced the bankruptcy

However, as this book graphically demonstrates, the two factors cited by Grinstein are merely the proximate cause for the bankruptcy filing.

Leadership decisions by Delta's Board and CEOs over a long period of years laid the foundation for Delta to be in a position where those two factors would have a large enough impact to result in bankruptcy.

A fundamental strategic factor was Delta's management discounting the potential effect of deregulation in 1978.

By promoting Ron Allen to CEO, primarily because he had moved up the chairs in the company through Beebe's efforts, the Board showed their lack of awareness of the need for a strategist to deal with the fundamental changes taking place in the airline industry.

Allen had smart people, some who demonstrated strong strategic ability reporting to him, but the boss was the one who needed to have it. He talked a lot about low cost carrier competition in annual reports while spending too much money instead of controlling and reducing costs so Delta could be more competitive.

Then the Board brought in Leo Mullin and gave him free rein for 6 ½ years to turn a cash rich company into one in such poor shape financially that his successor had to turn to expensive sources of money to keep the company afloat. Bankruptcy was only 20 months later.

Blaming fuel prices and low cost carriers for Delta's bankruptcy is like putting one's parents in a nursing home that did not properly care for them and then complaining about being an orphan after they are gone.

Blaming external factors is an excuse

The leadership lesson here is simply blaming external factors for failure is an excuse, not a reason, when a leader has had many opportunities and the control to make decisions in the past that either would have blunted or negated the effect of the external factors.

The lesson is even more emphatic when a leader has experience or information that, if properly used, should have clearly led to decisions protecting the company from harm.

For example, the airline industry has traditionally experienced fuel price crises periodically. Common sense would indicate such crises are likely to reoccur and, as a result, factor that into any strategic decision.

Prior to Ron Allen, Delta tightened their corporate belt continually to minimize the potential hit from the virtually certain periodic tough times. Under Robert Oppenlander, and the CEO's during his 30 years at Delta, the company exhibited the financial discipline to produce consistent profits and minimize the pain even during a brief period of losses. In fact, Delta was in such good shape financially that it was able comfortably to give employees 8% raises in the down year of 1982.

As interviewees commented repeatedly, financial discipline was not one of Allen's strong suits.

When Mullin took over, the Board gave the outsiders access to a very full, tasty cookie jar that they systematically and fully depleted.

The Mullin crowd's lack of knowledge of the airline business and their perceived lack of concern for

Delta's long-term financial health resulted in decisions that were key contributors to Delta's bankruptcy.

They blamed external factors, specifically the 9/11/2001 terrorist attacks, for Delta's weakened financial condition at the time.

While those attacks clearly hurt every airline, Delta's financial breathing room to deal with the after-effects had previously been curtailed by Mullin's management. Their decisions after the attack, with Board support, exacerbated Delta's problems.

By the time Mullin and his crowd were ushered out the door, Grinstein took over a company constrained by very narrow financial boundaries and had little room to maneuver. When confronted with the recent fuel crisis, Delta was then almost completely at the mercy of that external event.

Grinstein a conundrum

Conundrum, one of Federal Reserve chief Alan Greenspan's favorite terms, applies to something that is a riddle or difficult to explain.

It is very hard to understand how Grinstein, a person who has been so instrumental in allowing or creating the conditions for Delta's near death experiences, can now behave like a leader who understands, appreciates and wants to help Delta survive and prosper.

What makes his past actions at Delta even harder to understand is that he knows the industry; understands people; understands Delta's traditions and culture; has good people skills; and has demonstrated he knows how to run and lead a successful business.

Grinstein's primary responsibility for Delta's condition

The one constant in Delta leadership at the top, aside from Board member Edward Budd who joined in 1985, during the 18 years between Dave Garrett's retirement and today has been Gerald Grinstein.

Therefore, many believe, and I concur, that if any one person were selected as having primary responsibility for Delta's seriously weakened condition on January 1, 2004 and today, it would be Grinstein.

- Grinstein became a Delta Board member in 1987 after its merger with Western Airlines, which he previously headed and had restored to profitability before the merger

- Reportedly, he declined the offer to be Delta's CEO at the time of the merger

- During Ron Allen's tenure, he was an active Board member, either allowing or supporting Allen's decisions while apparently going along with the extensions of Allen's contract as CEO, even during the 4 years of major losses at Delta

- He led the charge to replace Allen but then led Delta "out of the frying pan and into the fire" in recruiting Leo Mullin, who arguably should never been given serious consideration for the job of CEO

- He was part of a Board that allowed Mullin and his crowd to make financial decisions and commitments that contributed to Delta being on the financial ropes now

- He was on the Board's Personnel & Compensation Committee when it approved the Mullin team's proposal for the *Executive Compensation Fiasco*

- He was on the Board's Personnel & Compensation Committee when it recommended extension of Mullin's contract, although Delta had already begun to get into serious financial trouble

- He remained silent after the *Executive Compensation Fiasco* became public

- When the retired Delta senior executive group identified the inequity of the pension treatment of Mullin's crowd compared to theirs, before it became public knowledge, Mullin's team was allowed to try to create an impression the retirees were the greedy ones. When the retirees later saw Delta's disastrous 2002 financial results, they withdrew their request for equity and instead requested Delta rescind the millions in pension trust payments to Mullin's crowd; this request was denied

- As part of a Board that held an abbreviated stockholder meeting immediately after the disclosure without an opportunity for stockholder questions (the Board was ushered out a side door to a private luncheon), he reinforced the growing perception that the *Executive Compensation Fiasco* was simply executive greed

- He supported Mullin after this public disclosure had effectively removed Mullin's ability to lead Delta and seriously damaged its credibility with all constituents - Washington, Atlanta community, customers, employees and stockholders

- By allowing Mullin to stay on as a lame-duck CEO for almost 18 months after the public disclosure of the *Executive Compensation Fiasco*, presumably so Mullin (and perhaps Grinstein) could save face, he effectively deprived Delta of a leader that the company sorely needed to deal with its millions in ongoing losses

- By allowing Mullin to continue making half-hearted non-apology apologies, the harmful aftermath of the disclosure was prolonged and more damaging to Delta

- By never admitting, in a straightforward and public manner, that he and the Board had made serious mistakes by hiring Mullin, supporting his actions and allowing him to linger, Grinstein reinforced his role as the one primarily responsible for Delta's dramatic decline

Jerry Grinstein's superlative leadership performance as Delta's CEO for 20 months is a dramatic and arguably amazing contrast to his prior performance documented above.

Delta's employee pensions a priority

During his time as CEO prior to the bankruptcy filing, Grinstein consistently demonstrated he clearly understands the high importance to the company of maintaining Delta's employee pension plan and its integrity.

Fight for Survival

Delta's two bankrupt mainline competitors, United and U.S. Airways (as of this writing soon to merge with America West, which only avoided bankruptcy in 2002 through a Federal loan guarantee), in bankruptcy have already walked away from their pension obligations.

These obligations have been turned over to the Pension Benefit Guaranty Corporation (PBGC), set up by Congress to insure that employees are not left without a pension should their company go bankrupt and walk away from pension commitments.

The problem is that PBGC is itself technically bankrupt with billions of dollars more in obligations than they have resources to fund. The current deficit is approximately $23.5 billion.

The funding for PBGC comes from "premiums," much like an insurance premium, that companies with pension plans are required by law to pay to PBGC. These premiums have been inadequate.

If more companies throw their pension obligations onto PBGC, it may run out of money. Many have a concern over a potential PBGC failure with the taxpayer ultimately bearing the burden.

The problem began when the entire U.S. steel industry went bankrupt a few years ago, turning over billions in obligations to PBGC. When United recently shedded $6.8 billion of unfunded obligations to PBGC, it set a new record as the largest. Bethlehem Steel set the previous record, $3.2 billion, in 2002.

A retired Bethlehem Steel executive, one of the interviewees, has been getting his regular pension check for about two years from PBGC. The situation is so fluid and PCGC in such disarray that these checks are coming with the express caveat from PBGC that the retiree must pay back the difference between what he has received and what PBGC eventually determines he should have received. This uncertainty means that he and the other Bethlehem retires have no idea how much of the check they receive should be saved for eventual repayment and when they will know.

By law each year the maximum benefit PBGC can pay is set under ERISA (Employee Retirement Income and Security Act). Currently, the maximum annual benefit they will pay, without regard to what the employee was supposed to receive, is $45, 526 a year for workers who retire at age 65. This means that a highly paid front line worker and an experienced manager or executive is likely facing significant cuts in their pension payments if PBGC takes over their company's plan.

By turning over their pensions to PBGC, two main competitors have already taken a major step toward reducing their costs. This obviously puts Delta at a competitive cost disadvantage. With mainline competitor Northwest now also in bankruptcy, Delta is potentially facing another airline with costs lowered by shedding their employee pension obligations.

Delta stops pension plan payments

One of Delta's first moves after bankruptcy filing was to announce the company would not make the $150 million pension plan payment due before the end of 2005. Delta also announced the company would stop funding the supplemental pensions for pilots and executives.

The irony is that every employee and retiree in the "Delta family" now has a major portion or all of their pensions in jeopardy – except those who were primarily responsible for creating the problem - Mullin, his senior executives and Ron Allen

PBGC's response to Delta's action was a statement on their web site which said, "Nothing in the bankruptcy code requires companies to skip their pension funding payments...They have a legal obligation to meet their funding requirements."

Initial reaction to Delta's statement from retiree groups and employees was dismay.

As one interviewee said, "So, while Leo and his departed team count their sleight-of-hand Delta-derived millions, long-time employees struggle with yet another pay cut and reduced benefits. Retirees (you know, the ones whose years of sweat and toil made the millions available for Leo and his team to cart out the door) sit in helpless fear of their pensions being erased."

The memory of the greed of Mullin and his crowd is on top of the minds of the legislators now being asked to help with the pension problem. Like the Energizer™ bunny, Leo just keeps going and going and going in his harm to the "Delta family."

Asking Congress for pension relief

Grinstein, along with non executive Board Chairman Jack Smith, former CEO of General Motors, and Scott Yohe, Delta's Washington representative (now retired but remaining as a consultant), have worked hard to get temporary pension relief for Delta. They are trying to facilitate the passage of a bill in Congress designed to lengthen the time any airline has to make up the underfunding of it pension obligations from 5 years to 25 years.

This would reduce the immediate cost and cash drain on Delta and give it more breathing room to work toward profitability. Originally, the hope was that such a bill would help preclude bankruptcy. Now the hope is it would help Delta get out of bankruptcy more quickly.

The argument for the legislation is that it would help airlines be in a better position to deliver promised pension benefits and not pass unfunded pension liabilities on to PGBC. The goal is to help ensure that the airline will pay benefits people have earned without a government bailout that might eventually cost taxpayers money.

The bill is entitled Employee Pension Preservation Act of 2005 (EPPA). U.S. Senator Johnny Isakson (R-GA) and Senator John D. Rockefeller IV (D-WV) introduced Senate Bill S. 861 on April 20, 2005. Hearings on the bill began quickly after that. Grinstein has already testified in a Senate committee hearing about the need for passage of the bill.

Grinstein reported to stockholders at the Delta annual meeting in May 2005 that Delta has experienced a warm and favorable reception to the bill from Congress. Northwest and Continental support the bill; however, American opposes it, presumably because they do not feel they need it now and want to prevent Delta and the other two supportive mainline carriers from getting any advantage over American.

Rep. John Boehner, R-Ohio, on June 15, 2005, introduced in the U.S. House of Representatives a substantially different pension reform bill. That bill is a more comprehensive approach to the problem of underfunding pension plans. It specifically does not provide the immediate relief sought by airlines. However,

Boehner had indicated he would "work with them (the airline industry) on pension reform."

On July 22, 2005, two key Senators on the Finance Committee – Grassley and Baucus – introduced another pension bill. Other Senators, including Kennedy, have said they are working on their own pension bills for possible introduction. The net effect of all this effort is confusion and no one law around which the politicians and businesses can rally.

Further delaying the discussion and eventual passage of a bill that might provide Delta pension relief has been Washington politicians' focus on the Hurricane Katrina response and the hearings on the nomination of Judge John Roberts for Chief Justice of the U.S. Supreme Court.

Now that Delta and Northwest have declared bankruptcy, some observers believe this might increase the pressure on Congress to move quickly to address the pension underfunding issue.

As this book went to press, committees in the U.S. Senate had reached a compromise to allow airlines an extension to 14 years to have their pension plans fully funded. The bill was scheduled for an early vote in the full Senate.

However, it does not look promising for Delta, which wanted 25 years. Even that long an extension Grinstein has said might not have been enough to insure Delta's survival.

Most of the provisions in the Senate bill would not take effect until 2007 although Delta needs relief right now.

The U.S. House of Representatives is working on its own pension bill with a vote tentatively scheduled for late October.

Even if both bills pass, additional time will be required for the two houses to work out the differences between their two bills before any relief measures could become law.

Engaging loyal Delta retirees

In a demonstration of his remarkable people skills and his ability to earn trust and respect, Grinstein successfully engaged Delta employees and particularly Delta retirees in an orchestrated lobbying effort to support passage of the Isakson/Rockefeller bill. Specifically, in spring 2005 he enlisted support from:

Delta Pioneers, group of over 9.000 Delta retirees, spouses and employees with at least 20 years service under the leadership of an advisory board, including Pat Malone

Delta Pilots Pension Preservation Organization (DP3) chaired by Jim Gray, a retired Delta captain

DALRC Retirement Committee that represents 5,000 Delta retirees and chaired by retiree Cathy Cone

All these retiree groups have a membership that loves Delta. They were part of helping build the company into the once financially solid organization that delivered fine customer service for decades. They understand Mr. Woolman's **"Service and Hospitality From The Heart"** for they lived it, breathed it and performed it every day. It is in their DNA.

This resource of thousands of loyal, competent Delta family members was largely untapped, if not ignored, under Mullin. Grinstein, in a dramatic 180° reversal, not only recognizes their importance in the family history but also engaged them in the pension initiative that is crucial to these family members and also the company.

By this action, he went a long way toward defusing the negative feelings against Delta management that festered and built up for years and then turned them around with a positive, collaborative effort.

As this book goes to press, it remains to be seen whether any bill will be introduced this year, much less passed.

It also remains to be seen how far the support of Grinstein by Delta's retiree groups will go now that Delta, after declaring bankruptcy, will not make the remaining pension payment due in 2005.

I hope that Grinstein, the bankruptcy judge and the creditors' committee appreciate the serious, permanent damage they will do to Delta's viability and future success were the pensions to be eliminated.

2005 "The Year of Delta's People"

In his remarks at the Delta annual shareholders' meeting on May 19, 2005, Grinstein reviewed the accomplishments Delta people had achieved in the face of adversity. Based on this, Grinstein dedicated 2005 as 'The Year Of Delta's People'. The specific accomplishments he cited were:

- *Taking $2 billion in costs out in one year without sacrificing revenue.* Grinstein appears to have integrity so it is reasonable the number he cited is based in fact and is significant. However, it was not reflected yet on the 2004 Profit & Loss Statement. Delta's operating expenses in 2004 were $18.3 billion compared to $14.9 billion in 2003, for an increase of $3.4 billion or 22.8%. Based on the reported financial statements, annual operating revenues in 2004 were $15.0 billion compared to $14.1 billion in 2003, Mullin's last year as CEO, for an increase of $900 million or 6.4%.

- *Improving Delta customer satisfaction, as measured by the highly regarded J.D. Power survey, at the same time costs were being taken out.* Delta was ranked #3 in the industry, ahead of all network carriers and surpassed only by the low cost/low fare airlines Southwest and JetBlue.

Delta's Transformation Plan

Grinstein commissioned the development of a comprehensive plan for Delta's survival and return to profitability in early 2004, immediately after he became CEO.

While Grinstein deserves commendation for involving Delta people in the development of this plan, I believe the process took entirely too long for a company that was in dire financial straits that were becoming more serious each day.

As I watched the plan development process unfold, I had two thoughts.

The first was here is a CEO finally who understands that a Delta people have a contribution to make in addressing its problems and treats their knowledge and experience with the respect it deserves.

Yet I was disturbed from the beginning at what seemed to me to be a serious lack of urgency under the circumstances. It had never made sense that Grinstein allowed eight months for the plan to be developed.

Taking that long seemed to indicate either the plan process was flawed or there was a problem with knowledge of those doing it. My instinct tells me that it took that much time because the person responsible for managing plan development was a former consultant with a large firm.

Large management consulting firms, from my observations, tend to create projects that take far longer than necessary; require excessive people; demand too many client resources to develop and implement; as a result, cost excessively much.

It may be an elegant plan conceptually to a strategist. However, it was too late and failed to keep Delta out of bankruptcy. I believe an important part of the reason Delta is now in bankruptcy is the excessive time it took to put together the plan while Delta bled.

Of immediate concern to me, as a stockholder and member of the "Delta family", is the person reportedly responsible for the plan is now Chief Operating Officer of Delta and rumored to be in line to succeed Grinstein.

Key Transformation Plan elements

Eight months later, in August 2004, **Delta's Transformation Plan** was completed and approved. Implementation began immediately and is still in process. Major plan elements were:

- **Simplifares** – This program totally repriced Delta, resulting in a few easily understandable fares replacing the traditional unwieldy patchwork of fare and a one-way domestic fare price cap of $499. The program was tested in 2004 in Cincinnati and rolled out systemwide in January 2005, based on positive test results. Grinstein attributed the customer satisfaction improvements in 2005 partly to the repricing. He also indicated it helped reduce costs by lowering pressure on reservation agents and encouraging more passengers to book on the company web site, the least cost distribution method for Delta.

- **Operation Clockwork** – On January 31, 2005, 51% of the Delta flights were rescheduled, a mammoth undertaking and arguably the most complex one day rescheduling in the history of the airline industry. This schedule restructuring converted Hartsfield-Jackson International Airport, Delta's main hub, into a continuous 24-hour operation. This initiative was essential to complement Simplifares so that Delta can provide service that is more reliable. This piece was considered important to retain those customers drawn to the airline or enticed back by the new pricing. Because of the more efficient operation, Delta gained the equivalent of 22 new aircraft with no capital investment.

- **Reaching agreement on a revised contract with the pilots' union ALPA**

(Air Line Pilots Association). The pilots agreed to take a major pay cut and changes in work rules. According to the company, this new contract produced a cost savings to Delta of $1 billion a year.

- Pay changes and longer workdays for everyone with the airline
- Cabin conditioning program that not only has contributed to higher customer satisfaction but also helped reduce fuel costs due to lighter weight seats
- Expansion of international flights
- Progress in the effort with Congress to provide temporary pension underfunding relief as detailed above
- **Increase in membership (Aeroflot and China Southern) to the international SkyTeam Alliance**
- **Introduction of a new advertising program with the theme "Good Goes Around"** to help recapture and communicate, internally and externally, the service spirit, teamwork and customer focus of Delta (recalling the foundation and legacy from Mr. Woolman and striving to rekindle the faintly flickering flame left by Mullin)

Challenges facing Delta on the road ahead enumerated by Grinstein at the May 19 meeting included:

Pensions – Delta is trying to retain the integrity of their employee pensions in contrast to United and U.S. Airways. The success of the effort in Washington to spread out company payments to the plan is seen by Grinstein as a key factor. As of the meeting, Delta had already contributed $220 million of the $450 million in pension plan contributions necessary in 2005.

Costs in general – Grinstein has asked the management team and all employees to scrutinize every aspect of the business to ask the questions, "Are we better off or worse off by doing this" and "Is there a better way to handle this?" His stated goal is for the company to take out an additional $1 billion in costs before the end of 2006.

Fuel – Delta Transformation Plan developed by Grinstein and his team assumed oil at $40 - $50 a barrel. He said that Delta was very close to being on plan (the recovery effort) in the first quarter of 2005; the plan was missed due to higher fuel costs at $50 - $60 a barrel.

Continuous improvement – Grinstein wants everyone in the company to look at their job and ask how it can be done better; how they can make a difference in the outcome; how can it be done more efficiently and productively. He views the job of leadership "to create an environment where that is not threatening but encouraging and everyone is on the same page and heading in the same direction."

Industry consolidations and mergers – Grinstein stated that none of these should be prejudged. His standard for whether the consolidation of other carriers will be good for Delta and the industry is whether it reduces the industry's excess capacity. (Subsequent to the meeting, America West announced a merger with U.S. Airways.) He said, "Strength in an airline is going to be measured by their ability to control or influence pricing and at the moment network carriers do not have that control in the marketplace."

He concluded his remarks by emphasizing the enormous changes that have taken place in the year since the last meeting and by paying tribute to the Delta people for bringing about these changes.

Major hurdles ahead

Grinstein and his team have major challenges to face as they climb what is clearly a very steep mountain to restore Delta to the pre-Mullin financial viability.

Grinstein predicated his Transformation Plan on crude oil prices remaining between $40 and $50 a barrel.

However, crude prices rose to $50 and stayed there for weeks. They exceeded $60 for the first time ever on June 27, 2005. In early September in intraday trading prices topped $70, but have settled down to remain consistently in the mid- to high $60's range.

Noted independent analyst Martin Weiss and Larry Edelson, his energy specialist associate, on July 1, 2005 correctly predicted $70 oil within a few weeks of that date and $100 and beyond in 2006. Weiss and Edelson two years ago accurately predicted the $60 oil we now have seen. If they are correct, then Delta and the entire airline industry will face record high fuel costs for the foreseeable future.

Anyone with experience in strategic planning knows to base a plan on a set of assumptions, as Delta did here, and possible alternate scenarios.

Then there must be an assessment of the probability that each alternate scenario might occur. Any alternate scenario with a strong probability should have a contingency plan. The contingency plan determines in advance how the company will respond to the alternate scenario should it occur. Instead of having to start from scratch to deal with the changed circumstances, a contingency plan can go into place immediately, blunting or negating the effects of those circumstances.

Delta made logical fuel cost assumptions when management created their plan. I do not know whether they looked at alternate, higher cost assumptions, but it would have been prudent to do so.

For example, known factors at the time of plan creation that had significant potential to increase fuel prices beyond Delta's assumptions were the uncertainty in the Middle East and the increasing worldwide demand for oil, driven particularly by China.

It appears to me that Delta had no contingency plan. The problem for Grinstein and team again was their lack of maneuvering room because of the serious financial condition of the company when he took over as CEO.

They may have avoided a contingency plan for $70+ oil out of concern the implication could be bankruptcy or dissolution.

Is airline industry sustainable at $70+ oil?

Recently departed Delta CFO Michael Palumbo, in his remarks to the Bear Stearns Global Transportation Conference on May 13, 2005, stated that it was unlikely any airline model (including low cost carriers) was sustainable if crude oil prices stayed above $50 a barrel.

CEO Grinstein echoed this view in his remarks at the May 19, 2005 shareholders' meeting.

Fight for Survival

Grinstein's supporting example was low-cost carrier Southwest, which had a profit of approximately $75 to $76 million in the first quarter of 2005; however, their profits from fuel hedging were $155 million. Grinstein's point was that running the airline cost Southwest $80 million for the quarter.

Since those statements were made, the low-cost carriers are surviving just fine and appear to be able to continue doing that.

The real question is can Grinstein and the Delta Board develop a plan that will enable Delta to survive at $70+ oil.

Importance of fuel hedging

Although it clearly will not insure profitability, the ability to hedge fuel has become a crucial survival tactic for airlines in the current and foreseeable environment.

Unfortunately, for Delta and the Grinstein team, they had to sell Delta's long-range fuel hedging contracts after taking over in early 2004 due to the poor cash position in which Mullin left the company.

By contrast, British Airways, according to Smart-Money.com, has locked in 60% of its fuel costs at $40 a barrel through March 2006 and is 20% hedged at $44 a barrel for the subsequent 12 months. Ireland-based low cost airline Ryanair for the 6 months through March 2006 hedged their fuel at $47 a barrel.

Joe Kolshak, Delta's Senior Vice President and Chief of Operations, sent a memo to the company's employees on June 30, 2005 outlining the company's strategies to fight the rising fuel prices. It is clear from the memo that a considerable amount of thought and effort has gone into developing and implementing the strategies. Among the strategies listed was a new short-term fuel hedging program that locked in roughly 10% of the airline's June 2005 fuel requirements.

Kolshak's memo also documented the results and successes the strategies are achieving. His memo is another demonstration of the top-notch business and communications skills for which he has become known. Kolshak joined Delta after stints as a Marine pilot, regional sales manager and then as an entrepreneur. After serving as Delta's Chief Pilot he moved to the business side as Director of Shareholder Relations. Kolshak was instrumental in helping Grinstein successfully negotiate the important new contract with the pilots' union, ALPA, in 2004.

The Kolshak document is an example of Delta striving mightily now to leverage its cash and other resources as much as is humanly possible.

Capitalization and access to capital

Under Mullin, Delta's market capitalization, or market cap, (the publicly traded share price multiplied by the number of shares outstanding) increased from 1997 to 2000. It hit a high of around $70 a share (about $140 a share before a 2:1 split).

Then it began a dramatic decline until Grinstein took over in 2004; the market cap decline continued, primarily because of the airline's declining financial performance.

As recently as May 2005 Delta stock was selling for $4.30 a share; these shares are now worth about $.70 - $.80 each.

Fight for Survival

For a company in bankruptcy, where Delta is now, the common stock often drops to a small price or becomes completely worthless

A company's market cap is important because it is an indicator of how the financial markets view the value and viability of the company. This affects access to traditional capital markets and the terms on which the company has access to capital.

Delta has had to go to expensive, non-traditional sources of capital in the last 18 months – structuring deals with American Express and GE with tough terms for Delta.

Comparative market cap figures on July 1, 2005 demonstrate not only Delta's difficult position at that time but also that of the mainline carriers in general.

The market cap of the low cost carriers, all with much lower revenues than either Delta or Northwest, was substantially higher. In fact, the market cap of Delta, Northwest, or United (which was in bankruptcy at the time) was much less than AirTran, although AirTran had less than 8%, 10% and 7% respectively of the three larger carrier's revenues.

The market cap of Continental, which is 9 times larger than AirTran in revenues, was only 10.8% larger than AirTran's.

Southwest had a far larger market cap than all the other airlines listed combined.

Access to capital has become a key issue for Delta as well.

The July 1, 2005 issue of the Wall Street Journal ran a story about investments in bonds of airlines and the risks associated with that investment.

It stated that the unsecured bondholders of U.S. Airways Group Inc. that filed Chapter 11 bankruptcy in September, 2004 (and is now slated for acquisition by America West) ended up getting just 1.2 ¢ on the dollar from their investment.

Many bond investors now are purchasing only airline bonds that are secured by assets, for example, equipment trust certificates. The Journal stated that higher quality certificates (those that give the bondholder guaranteed coupon payments for 18 months in the event of bankruptcy) are yielding 6.50% to 7.00% while yields of lower quality instruments are between 8.00% and 9.00%. These are high yields and the coupon payments are a cash drain on the already cash strapped carriers.

Employees taking another salary hit

Leadership 7.5 supposedly created billions of dollars in ongoing savings for Delta. Mullin's cuts were supposed to create billions of additional savings. Then Grinstein's Transformation Plan was supposed to create billions more in savings.

The cumulative result of all this "savings" has been thousands of people without a job, tens of thousands of people with their pensions at serious risk and a company in bankruptcy – and wealthy retired CEOs.

Immediately after the bankruptcy filing, additional salary cuts were announced:

- CEO   25%
- Officers   15%
- Merit employees   9%
- Flight attendants 9-10%

Fight for Survival

- ACS and reservations   9%
- AMTs   7%

The reduced salaries of the top executives are now: Grinstein - $337,500; COO and CFO - $382,500 each; 4 other top executives - $344,250.

In my opinion, if Grinstein and his team think that their taking a larger percentage (on paper) cut than the rest of the employees somehow magically will now create a feeling of "shared pain" in the Delta tradition, he is out of touch with reality.

For example, a very good, senior flight attendant I know will have their pay cut from approximately $50,000 a year to about $36,000 after January 1. This pay cut will result from a combination of the percentage cut and changed work rules.

My calculator says that flight attendant will be taking a 28% pay cut, a greater percentage than Grinstein's 'company leading' 25% cut.

The impact on the flight attendant's life style will be dramatic, but barely significant to the officers. There are many other employees making less money than this flight attendant who will be impacted even worse.

The point here is not that management is in a position to maintain salaries. Due to past CEO and Board leadership failures documented in this book, they now have no choice but to cut.

However, I suggest they not insult the intelligence of Delta people by trying to create the impression the top people are experiencing pain to a greater degree than, or even remotely comparable to, the people on the front line.

Assessment of Grinstein's performance

Grinstein, when he became CEO of Delta, assumed primary responsibility for a patient that many viewed as being in the Intensive Care Unit.

He has led a mighty effort to try to treat the patient so it could be moved from ICU to a regular ward and eventually released from the hospital.

Instead, the patient is now in the emergency room, bankruptcy, on life support.

For all his effort as CEO, Grinstein bears a heavy share of the responsibility for the decisions that contributed to Delta ending up in the emergency room.

A friend once advised me, "No one is responsible for the cards they were dealt, only for the way they play them." However, Jerry Grinstein has to play cards in a lousy hand that he helped deal himself. Unfortunately, tens of thousands of employees, retirees, families and other members of the "Delta family" are also faced with playing that lousy hand as well.

The front page of "Atlanta Journal-Constitution" on 9/15/2005, the day following the filing, quoted Grinstein, "...fuel, fuel, fuel was the killer for us."

I say **"leadership, leadership, leadership" was the killer for Delta**.

Now we will see if leadership can revive and heal the patient.

Strategic and specific suggestions on how to do that are in the next chapter.

8 – Delta's Bankruptcy

Jerry Grinstein has repeatedly committed to transforming and reinvigorating Delta Air Lines. First, he must insure its survival. To accomplish that, he must successfully bring it through bankruptcy.

Not so fast, Jerry

As this book was going to press, I learned Grinstein reportedly is now in the office only about a week a month. This absence may be understandable if it has been on Delta business. However, if it is an indication he is trying to slip quietly out the door, I believe many will contend he is shirking his duty. The reasons for that statement follow.

Emerging from bankruptcy successfully

In this chapter I offer strategic and tactical suggestions from the head and the heart – both as a "Delta family" member and a management consulting professional – that I believe will improve Delta's probability of emerging from bankruptcy successfully.

My definition of success for Delta is remaining an independent, profitable company that reflects the values on which the company built its prior success for decades.

I fervently hope that all those charged with saving Delta will consider these suggestions along with the leadership lessons throughout the book. While I make no claim to infallibility, I have done my homework for this book thoroughly and also have a track record of being right a lot more often than being off target.

I also hope that this book will help all those who have a role in Delta's bankruptcy, particularly those who are less familiar with the company, to understand Delta's uniqueness while they are making the necessary financial computations and decisions.

My direct style is intentional. It is what CEOs tell me they value about working with me. Delta certainly needs directness now. There is no time for pleasantries.

Grinstein must stay as CEO

Jerry Grinstein must stay as CEO until Delta gets out of bankruptcy, notwithstanding his age and his self-imposed term limit (which was 3 years from 1/1/2004 at one point and then became 2).

He may be the only leader on the horizon, in my opinion, who has the capability of leading Delta successfully through the troubled waters of bankruptcy.

Grinstein is a one-man case history of the importance of picking the right CEO.

He has a unique combination of assets that Delta sorely needs to retain:

- Demonstrated ability to lead
- Knowledge of the airline business
- Knowledge of Delta
- Experience as CEO
- Credibility with Delta stakeholders
- Legal training and experience
- Experience in dealing with complex financial transactions

If Grinstein completely turned over the reins now it would be a step backwards for the company.

Delta can ill afford any glitches during this critical juncture in its history and needs the best leader.

Grinstein has an obligation to stay

I believe Jerry Grinstein has an obligation to stay as CEO of Delta until Delta is able to climb out of bankruptcy.

Because of his intimate involvement, at the Board level and recently as CEO, with every major issue and decision at Delta since 1987, Grinstein is accountable for Delta's dire circumstances now.

He not only has a fiduciary responsibility to Delta for helping fix the problems, but also an ethical responsibility.

During his time as CEO, Grinstein has behaved like a man of integrity. He has been candid and realistic in his assessments. He has communicated these assessments and his decisions and those of the Board very effectively.

However, after being such an integral part of creating Delta's problems, it would frankly be unconscionable for him to walk out the door now, leaving Delta "holding the bag".

To leave with an untested replacement would evade his personal and professional responsibility to a company and tens of thousands of "Delta family" members.

Selling out Delta is not the answer

Grinstein has been CEO of two companies when they merged, so he knows how to lead a company to a "transaction" as the merger and acquisition people call it.

I believe that proper leadership can guide Delta successfully from bankruptcy.

I believe I also reflect the views of many when I say that if Grinstein leads Delta to a "transaction" where the company name and culture no longer exists, then he will have copped out of directly solving a mess he contributed to creating.

Were there a "transaction," he would achieve his personal goal of getting back to Seattle, but leave 100,000 "Delta family" members in his dust.

Leadership, leadership, leadership not fuel, fuel, fuel

He does not get off the hook by saying, "...fuel, fuel, fuel..." brought Delta to its knees as Grinstein was quoted in the headline on the front page of the Atlanta Journal-Constitution on the day following the bankruptcy filing.

Leadership brought Delta to its knees by allowing the company to get in such a position that an outside circumstance, granted an extreme one, could put the company in bankruptcy.

WHERE WAS THE BOARD and where was Jerry Grinstein over the last 18 years when Delta had the cash and financial stability to protect Delta from potentially devastating circumstances?

Jerry Grinstein needs to stand up to his obligations, stay in Atlanta and fix Delta.

In his bankruptcy email to employees, Grinstein said, "There have been other difficult times in Delta's history, and the company has always turned to its people..."

The above statement is quite true. Delta people have been the backbone of the company's performance in spite of the Board and CEO's.

It is now time for Delta people to be able to turn to Grinstein to lead the way out of difficult times he helped create.

They have a right to expect no less.

I believe that if Grinstein left without a fix and his successor was then unsuccessful, the failure of Delta Air Lines, Inc. should be laid appropriately and squarely at Jerry Grinstein's feet.

He would go down in airline history as the savior of Western Airlines and the architect of the demise of Delta.

Delta can ill afford another Ron Allen or Leo Mullin

Delta cannot withstand another mistake at the CEO level. The Board must find the best successor.

Grinstein has proven he can rekindle the Delta culture under extraordinary conditions. However, this rekindling is very fragile and most managers would be unable to sustain the momentum created by Jerry.

In July 2005, as part of a reorganization of his management team, Grinstein promoted a young man in his late 30's, to be Chief Operating Officer.

I share with others in the "Delta family" the strong concerns that Grinstein intends to make this fellow CEO soon, so Grinstein can walk out the door.

Like Allen in 1987, he is bright, but probably too young to have the maturity and wisdom that generally comes with age. Allen was Delta's Chief Operating Officer prior to Delta's Board making him CEO.

Although the PR following this young man's promotion announcement seemed to put a spin on the individual as 'old Delta', the fact is he only joined the company in 2002. His previous experience was with a large management consulting firm where he was on a team working with Delta for about 2 years prior to Delta hiring him.

The greatest concern is that, prior to joining Delta, he had no apparent experience in a senior executive role with a company of the size and scope of Delta.

Like Mullin, we have a former management consultant without a managerial track record, except the young man's managerial experience seems even thinner than Mullin's at the time Delta hired him.

In fairness, Grinstein credits the young man with playing a key leadership role in the development of the Transformation Plan.

However, as noted earlier, the plan took far too long to develop under Delta's circumstances at the time. In addition, it was predicated on a key assumption that proved to be quite inaccurate.

Those two factors were very instrumental in Delta having to file for bankruptcy.

Bankruptcy

The young man is reportedly quite bright and a good strategic thinker. He also has demonstrated his project management skills.

Those attributes would indicate an executive who can make a continuing contribution at Delta – but not as CEO – working under Jerry Grinstein's leadership.

If Grinstein were to give the huge CEO job to a business youngster with unproven leadership skills, he would be assuming Tom Beebe's role when he paved the way for Ron Allen to become CEO.

Grinstein's team and the Board would probably go along with him if he insisted, just as they did with Beebe. However, it would again be putting Delta at risk just to satisfy the boss.

Qualified candidate available for COO

It is difficult to understand why Grinstein did not make Joe Kolshak, Executive Vice President and Chief of Operations, the Chief Operating Officer.

Kolshak has far stronger executive credentials and a proven record of accomplishment compared to the young man who was given the promotion:

- Mental toughness of a former Marine fighter pilot
- Member of the "Delta family" for 17 years
- Heart that would make Mr. Woolman proud (see Letter 1 in the Appendix)
- Entrepreneurial ability and courage
- Has actually run a business and sold something to earn a living prior to joining Delta

- Proven managerial capability through a series of promotions in leadership positions at Delta
- Demonstrated financial expertise and people skills as Director – Investor Relations for Delta
- Excellent communications skills – both written and verbal
- Possesses common sense

These attributes seem to me far more predictive of a successful future CEO than those of Grinstein's COO now.

I understand there may ill feelings among some pilots toward Kolshak for his role in helping Delta negotiate the 2004 reductions in pilot compensation. The expression I heard was "some feel like he didn't look out for the pilots." In my opinion, the Mullin crowd had left the company in such bad shape that no one at that point, including pilot union leaders, was in a position to "look out for the pilots." I also believe a very small minority shares these ill feelings. Instead, any widespread ill feelings among pilots are directed where they belong, toward Mullin and prior Delta Boards of Directors.

Protect Delta's unique remaining asset

Although they have been kicked in the teeth repeatedly, as they are right now, the "Delta family" still has a residual affection and some even a passion for the company. (Please read the two letters in the Appendix.)

Anyone who has flown the other airlines now in bankruptcy knows that their employees rarely have these positive feelings for their company.

For example, Delta employees tangibly demonstrated their affection and passion in 1982 when they voluntarily initiated the collection of $30 million from their own pockets to buy an airplane for Delta, which was experiencing temporary financial difficulties. No other airline in history has had a relationship with its employees with the depth, breadth and strength of Delta Air Lines.

However, as one interviewee said, Mullin and Burns mortgaged that plane, aptly named "Spirit of Delta," for an equity line. Mullin not only damaged the culture but also mortgaged the most highly visible manifestation of the "Delta family" culture.

Although the passion has been badly damaged, it has not been destroyed. Even today, the DALRC has collected from Delta retirees, whose pensions have been put in jeopardy, over $13,000 for a fuel fund to help their beloved company deal with the high fuel prices.

Jerry Grinstein understands this dedication and says so often, including in his memorandum to employees announcing the bankruptcy filing.

His memo said, "In what is an enormous testament to Delta people and their strong commitment to customer service, during this same period of intense transformation, Delta was selected "Most Preferred" by business travelers, our SkyMiles program was voted best in a survey by Travel Savvy magazine, and our self-service kiosks were singled out as tops in the industry by an independent research firm."

He was referring to implementation of the Transformation Plan during which "we have undertaken cost-cutting initiatives and massive network, scheduling and operational improvements without adversely impacting our revenue-generating ability or our renowned customer service – a feat few have attempted and even thought possible."

I respectfully but strongly remind him and all those involved in the bankruptcy process, particularly those who deal primarily in numbers, that **Delta's greatest asset really is its people.**

Unique asset eroded and fragile but alive

As the book documents, the value of that asset has been severely eroded by decisions of the Board of Directors and CEOs in recent years.

It is a miracle it is still alive. I believe were it not for Mr. Woolman's powerful shadow and the values and love of Delta he instilled in those who followed, that asset would now be as worthless as Delta stock today.

Driven by that powerful legacy, Delta people, including some of their senior leaders, have persevered through much adversity to run as fine an airline as the Board and the CEO would allow.

Yet top-level decisions and circumstances over time have severely damaged the asset and it is now quite fragile.

I believe the asset is extremely vulnerable to the decisions stakeholders will make while Delta is in bankruptcy. If one or more of those decisions destroy the asset, it will be gone for good.

If the bean counters and moneychangers ignore the asset, they will cost themselves far more money than they might imagine.

Bankruptcy

Contrast between Delta and Northwest

My friends in the Midwest refer to Northwest disparagingly as "Northworst" because of their ongoing experience with that airline and its people.

The company's poor relationship with its employees reflects in its service.

After flying that airline on several occasions to client meetings in Wisconsin, I now understand how the airline earned it nickname.

The news reports of a possible merger between Delta and Northwest is alarming to me.

One of the harmful, long-term effects from Delta's purchase of Pan Am assets was the damage to Delta's culture from the negative attitudes of some of the Pan Am employees that joined Delta.

Delta survived the negative effects because the company's relationship with employees was still so strong.

Leadership 7.5 damaged the relationship between management and Delta employees. Then Leo Mullin and the *Executive Compensation Fiasco* dealt it a body blow. What happens beyond the bankruptcy filing has the potential to destroy it. A Northwest merger might be such a destroying event.

Contrast between Delta and American

American also has had a history of a terrible relationship with employees. Under Robert Crandall in the 1980's and Donald Carty in the late 1990's, the relationship was adversarial.

I had dinner several years ago, when Carty was still CEO, with the leaders at American of APFA, their flight attendant's union, and their entire contract negotiating team.

In all my years in business, I have never observed such mistrust of a company's management and antagonism toward it.

I got an earful of horror stories of management's, particularly Crandall's, demeaning attitudes, words and actions toward employees.

As previously noted, American's Board terminated Carty in March 2002, to control the public and employee relations damage from the disclosure of American's version of an *Executive Compensation Fiasco*. Like Leo Mullin, Carty secretly got millions for himself while he was publicly getting an agreement with employees to cut their income.

Gerard Arpey, who followed Carty, appears to have improved somewhat the relationship between American's management and employees.

Retain Delta's employee pension plan

This may seem counterintuitive, particularly since dumping their pension plans was one of the actions that United and U.S. Airways took in bankruptcy.

However, in the Delta culture it makes complete sense. Retaining the pension plan is essential to protect Delta's unique asset – the loyalty and affection members of the "Delta family" feel for the company.

Grinstein has done an outstanding job of rekindling the Delta culture following the erosion under Allen and the near death experience under Mullin. He has engaged the Delta retiree organizations to assist the company in support of the Employee Pension Preservation Act now before Congress.

Because of the Grinstein-led efforts to renew Delta's culture and preserve its pension plan, he has earned the admiration, respect and affection of a large number of employees and retirees.

For the moment, he has overcome the negative feelings that resulted from his support of Mullin and of the *Executive Compensation Fiasco* under Mullin.

If Grinstein can continue to preserve the pension plan in bankruptcy, he will likely go down in airline history as a remarkable man who successfully swam against the conventional wisdom.

On the contrary, I believe that if, in bankruptcy, he sacrifices Delta's pensions to the PBGC, then Grinstein will probably be regarded in the same vein as Mullin from then on. His considerable efforts up to now will be forgotten and the pension failure will be his legacy with employees and the industry.

Make "Service and Hospitality From The Heart" Delta's theme and mantra

Almost every interviewee had a strong, emotional and very positive reaction to that concept first espoused by Mr. Woolman decades ago. It has been decades since Mr. Woolman used them, but they rang true with everyone I interviewed.

These 6 words memorably and succinctly state the values on which Delta is based. They convey a focus on the customer <u>and</u> a focus on supporting fellow Delta team members. They particularly convey the commitment of management to support employees in serving the customer.

They also convey to the customer, as they always have, the commitment of Delta and its people to them.

The current "Good Goes Around" theme may work acceptably as an internal concept. However, I submit it is a far less compelling and memorable one, particularly for customers, than **"Service and Hospitality From The Heart"**.

Resurrecting the words of Mr. Woolman can be an important part of Mr. Grinstein's efforts to recapture the spirit of Delta. It conveys that the source of service to customers and to Delta team members must come from the inside – from the *heart*.

At the May 19, 2005 shareholders' meeting, Grinstein shared a very moving story about the teamwork and commitment involved in returning a passenger's computer to him promptly. He then said this was one of many stories like it and lamented that Delta did not do a better job of getting them out.

I suggest he go back and look at the **"We Love To Fly And It Shows"** television commercials from the late 1980's. Joining the creative concept of showing actual Delta people happily doing extraordinary things for customers in their jobs with the theme **"Service and Hospitality From The Heart"** would be a powerful combination.

These 6 words originally coined by Mr. Woolman epitomize what the Delta family followed to build the company and what many employees still believe and follow today. The overwhelming favorable reaction to these words from interviewees is strong evidence of their meaning, substance and power. They truly epitomize what Delta has been and strives to become again.

The spirit of Delta is still alive; the many documented cases of Delta's people going the extra mile must be communicated and capitalized on to demonstrate the living spirit to the customer and to boost employee morale as well.

Rehire BBDO as Delta's advertising agency

One of Ron Allen's last and lasting harmful acts to Delta was replacing Delta's advertising agency of 50 years.

It is ironic that the agency he fired is the same one that created the highly successful "We Love To Fly And It Shows" television commercials mentioned above.

Delta's advertising has never been quite the same. Delta has been with other local Atlanta agencies, gone to Chicago and New York.

None of BBDO's successors has captured Delta's uniqueness in the advertising they have produced as BBDO did consistently for decades.

My opinion of why BBDO was terminated, based on Allen's public comments at the time, is Allen's ego and its reflection on Delta. He thought that Delta was, using a classic Southern expression, "too big a dog" to have an agency that originated in Atlanta (Burke Dowling Adams was the original firm which sold out to BBDO and became their Atlanta office) when he had global aspirations for the airline.

One thing is sure. Delta, with BBDO's considerable assistance, made money throughout the entire relationship until Allen took over.

Some of the key players on the Delta account are still with the agency. They retain the institutional memory of Delta – and the appreciation and love of the company and its culture– that would get them up and running promptly.

Eliminate Human Resources

Interviewees most familiar with Delta currently cited this area as Delta's major weakness now.

The perception of the HR operation is one that is project oriented and not strategic. More than ever, Delta now needs a strategic HR function.

Most important, the leadership in this department has convinced Grinstein that they are the guardians of the Delta culture. In fact, interviewees repeatedly said that HR leadership instead has done major damage to the culture. Those who truly believe in and live the Delta culture have been systematically marginalized.

From what I have learned, Delta's HR has apparently become a closed loop, mutual admiration society with finely honed political instincts and the ability to create and deliver impressive PowerPoint presentations.

I am reminded of a situation at a private club where I am a member. For years, most members intensely disliked the General Manager because his behavior and the policies he advocated demonstrated a serious lack of regard for their preferences and interests. However, he was a master at cultivating favor with the club's Board. Only when a wise club president championed the development of a confidential member survey did this long-time situation become apparent. Soon after the results were published, the manager was replaced; he should have been replaced long before.

Replace HR with Strategic Culture leader

Grinstein needs someone in charge with integrity, good business judgment and particularly a strategic view of how to align effectively all the people in the company with the business strategy.

He also needs someone who has the skills to make sure Delta's retains its unique culture while the company and its employees deal with all the additional stresses that bankruptcy will produce.

I suggest Grinstein bring back Anthony Austin as Delta's Strategic Culturist.

Austin, in my opinion, was one of the few Delta executives brought in from outside during the Mullin era who has a respect and appreciation for Delta's tradition and culture.

In addition, he has the sorely needed, high-level experience in human resources organization of sophisticated, large companies. He is knowledgeable about the traditional human resources tools but has the mindset to use them strategically and cost effectively.

He impressed me as someone with the people and communications skills to use his expertise to address Delta's needs in a manner that Delta people would respect and willingly accept.

Austin would hit the ground running and make a major contribution to helping Delta get through bankruptcy and out of it successfully.

Turn loose and empower the Six Sigma people

An interviewee credited Delta executive Tony Charaf for introducing Delta to the Six Sigma continuous process improvement about 10 years ago and later the Lean process of eliminating waste and maximizing value.

As the reader may know, Six Sigma is the approach to delivering high quality products and services pioneered by Deming in the early 1980's.

When American companies dismissed Deming's ideas, he took them to the Japanese who embraced them. There he helped Japanese auto manufacturers develop higher quality products than those of U.S. companies. This changed forever the old image of Japanese products being shoddy and propelled Japanese cars to high sales worldwide.

After seeing the results of Deming's ideas with the Japanese, American companies started to embrace them.

I have personally seen and been part of Six Sigma transforming a major American corporation. Motorola was one of the first U.S. companies to embrace this concept throughout the enterprise. CEO Robert Galvin ran into considerable resistance from his top executives. As one of the steps to break down that resistance, I set up, throughout the country, focus groups of customers of all major Motorola product lines.

The unusual technique I used for these groups was to have the top executives of major areas of the company – for example, distribution and manufacturing – actually sit at the table with the respondents. They were observers, not participants, unless a customer raised an issue related to a particular executive's area of responsibility. At that point, I would then request the executive respond to the customer's concern directly and immediately before moving forward with the rest of the group.

It only took a half dozen cities of this experience to convince the reluctant executives of Motorola's need to improve quality dramatically. With this broad senior-level support, Mr. Galvin was then able to introduce Six Sigma throughout Motorola effectively.

For years in the late 1980's and early 1990's Motorola then became a corporate icon of quality.

Six Sigma is often misused

Like many popular business techniques, Six Sigma is often misused. After reading about its value to a Motorola or a GE, who embraced the technique and integrated it into their processes, many have merely dabbled with it while expecting the same dramatic results.

For example, several years ago, my wife and I decided to renovate our kitchen and den. We contracted with Expo, the upmarket division of Home Depot, to deliver us a 'turnkey' result – design, appliances, labor, materials, and project management – for a fixed price. After months of ongoing delays and foul-ups at Expo, they finally were near to completing the work. However, no one seemed to have any responsibility or accountability for finishing it.

I talked with Home Depot CEO, Bob Nardelli, and asked his advice. He referred me to the head of the Expo division, who was very apologetic and immediately acknowledged Expo had serious problems. Even with the two head people involved, to get the job completed took another three months – the planned total time frame for the entire job at the outset.

When it was over, I shared with the Expo head observations, as both a customer and a management consultant, on key strategic issues. He agreed with the observations.

He told me Expo was going to use Six Sigma to address those issues. When I asked him what customer information he was going to use to initiate the process, to my amazement, he said, "None. We are going to do it all with our own people internally."

I believed then that the process was doomed to failure at Expo. Six Sigma begins and ends with the customer.

Sitting around a conference table or in a meeting room with the same people who were part of creating the problem – and had demonstrated repeatedly over a period of months they were clueless about customers - is equivalent to staring at your navel awaiting a divine solution to a problem.

It was not surprising that a year later the Expo head was gone; Home Depot decided to deemphasize the Expo brand, abandoned all expansion plans and cut the number of existing stores.

Six Sigma at Delta

Delta has used Six Sigma but never really capitalized on it, in the opinion of some closest to the situation.

Charaf now has heavy responsibilities Senior Vice President – Technical Operations. He is in charge of the safety and maintenance of Delta's fleet of aircraft along with insuring compliance with FAA mandates. As part of Delta's cost restructuring, he has decided to outsource some of the work in his area and is now implementing that decision.

Therefore, I suggest Grinstein contract with Bill Kline, who retired as Delta's VP/Chief Learning Officer, to set up and manage a truly enterprise-wide Six Sigma effort to lead Delta's continuous process improvement while squeezing out costs.

Kline is another one of the few outsiders hired during the Mullin era who has a respect and appreciation for Delta's values and culture.

He is a very bright, has high energy and behaves with the utmost integrity.

My perception is that his high integrity and directness made him unpopular with other key HR leaders, some of whom are still at Delta.

He is an experienced Six Sigma black belt with broad credentials in working with and leading others in continuous improvement from his career at GE, one of the country's preeminent companies to use Six Sigma successfully.

To remove this operation from politics and personalities so they can be most effective for Delta, it must report directly to Grinstein.

What Delta does not need is a large management consulting firm bringing over a cast of thousands to make Six Sigma work at Delta.

Fire all the management consultants

Delta has spent millions with *Consultant X* alone plus a substantial amount with another large management consulting firm. In addition, Delta has been a proverbial gravy train for dozens of other consultants during the last 10 years.

As the bankruptcy shows, none of these firms has provided Delta the solution to its problems.

For that reason alone, Grinstein should terminate them.

Furthermore, Delta can no longer afford their services, unless of course they suddenly decide to work free. Even "free" work from the big firms is costly to the client. One of their standard marketing ploys is to offer a free mini-engagement. The purpose for the big firm generally is to get enough ammunition to support a proposal for a large project costing the client megabucks. Overworked client employees – fearing for their job if the consultant does get the large project – make their regular work a lower priority in order to meet the information needs of the consultant. The employee, the company and sometimes the customer suffer during this "free" work. Ultimately, the only one receiving benefit from this "free" work is the consulting firm. Every time I see this happening, I wonder when clients will finally wise up to the shenanigan.

Reportedly, one of the first management moves by Grinstein, when he took over as CEO in January 2004, was to terminate work with *Consultant X*.

By this decision, he eliminated a substantial on-going expense. He also earned the respect of many employees and executives who have seriously questioned the value of this firm to Delta as well as the value of other consulting firms hired by the company.

His later decision to rehire *Consultant X* was a disappointment to many.

Interviewees have told me many stories that demonstrate an apparent lack of appreciation or concern, from these firms, for the culture and values of Delta or for the long-term effect of their recommendations on the company.

My observations of typical large consulting firm behavior in other companies support this view.

Delta unable to afford management consultant cost or their demands on its people

In addition to the need to control costs, Grinstein is trying to keep Delta's culture alive. He can ill afford external - or internal - help that does not completely support that effort. It is fundamental to getting Delta out of bankruptcy and moving it forward from there.

Big firm strategy consultants, like the two Delta has been using, generally require a considerable amount of time from client employees to support the consultant's efforts.

In a company like Delta, which has already cut thousands of jobs but still has a demanding business to run, fewer employees must do more work, with little time left to help a consultant look good while doing their own day job.

In addition, because they are "boardroom consultants", they do not get their hands dirty in the mundane day-to-day world where their client's people live.

Therefore, once their high-level ideas are sold to the CEO and Board, these same overworked, stressed out client employees, must then implement them.

I hope Grinstein will provide Delta's long-suffering employees relief from this expensive millstone.

Control management consultant costs by requiring CEO and Board approval

My suggestion is that Grinstein follow the path of Stan Sigman, president and CEO of Cingular Wireless. Reportedly, Sigman, like Grinstein, terminated all the many existing consultant contracts when he took over as CEO in late 2002 after making it clear that he wanted his managers to be totally accountable for their performance.

Sigman then made a policy that no one could hire a consulting firm without the would-be hiring manager making a strong business case, including particularly the projected return on investment in the consulting fees. Sigman or his CFO must approve this case.

Since that policy decision, the only major management consulting contract at Cingular has been a short-term one to assist in the initial integration of AT&T Wireless after it was purchased in late 2004.

Once Grinstein has terminated all the consultants, then I suggest he set up a policy where an executive must make a business case directly to him prior to any future consulting engagements.

In addition, I suggest the Board set a policy that Delta's CEO must make a business case for their approval prior to any commitments to consultants, with the understanding that they will give any request given intense scrutiny.

Replace management consultants with retired Delta executives

This may appear counterintuitive. However, recall the evidence that these retired executives have been part of Delta's backbone and strength.

The leadership problem at Delta has been concentrated at the CEO level and with the Board.

Under an effective leader like Grinstein, these people would also be effective.

I know retired Delta executives who could come back in and hit the ground running – a characteristic Grinstein sorely needs. I am confident there are many more than the ones I know who would be effective contributors.

Delta already contracts with some recently retired executives to keep access to their skills set and their knowledge of the company.

What I suggest is a broad, coordinated strategic program to identify Delta's needs and then match them with retired executives.

Financially, this approach makes sense because Delta would get experienced talent for far less than the salary of a full-time hire, with no additional benefits or overhead costs.

These retired executives embrace the Delta culture and would be instrumental in helping Grinstein retain and expand it.

Furthermore, they would have a strong incentive to give their work their best effort, not only out of love for Delta but also to help protect their pensions by helping save Delta.

The Federal government has a program that utilizes retired executives on behalf of small businesses. The acronym is SCORE, which stands for Service Corps Of Retired Executives.

I propose Delta call its program **SCORED**, the acronym for **Service Corps Of Retired Executives Of Delta.**

This program will enable Delta to capitalize on one of its most underutilized assets – its retirees – to help bring the business back to solvency and then profitability.

To run SCORED, I suggest joint responsibility be given Maurice Worth and Bob Coggin. Both men are smart, proven executives who have the respect of many Delta retirees and a strong relationship with them that has continued into retirement.

They know the strengths and capabilities of a number of retired executives and how to find out the capabilities of those with whom they are personally unfamiliar.

They know first hand the strengths and weaknesses of Delta's Leadership 7.5 initiative, knowledge that would help Delta immediately as the company navigates through bankruptcy.

Bankruptcy

Three part bankruptcy strategy

To manage through the bankruptcy, I suggest a 3-part strategy:

- Ongoing operations
- Development of new business model
- Financial and legal

The current operating team can focus on running the airline.

SCORED would develop the new business model. Obviously, they will need input from the operating team. However, SCORED will not make the intense, ongoing demands on the operating team that the large management consulting firms make.

Finally, the financial and legal people will be responsible for the ongoing requirements of the bankruptcy process.

The heads of each of these three strategic groups would report to Grinstein who must retain the responsibility for the bankruptcy outcome.

Recognize that Delta's increased focus on international is a short-term fix

Develop now a strategy to compete against the coming low fare competition on international routes.

Right now international operations are the only place Delta is making money.

Delta has indicated recently that the company plans even greater focus on these more profitable routes. That makes common sense and strategic sense.

However, interviewees and press reports confirm that the trend to low-cost carriers, now confined primarily to the domestic market, is going to be a major factor in the international market in the not too distant future.

The leadership lesson from its history that Delta must not repeat is discounting the likelihood of low fare competition internationally as Delta did for many years domestically following deregulation in 1978. That oversight – and the lack of an effective, sustained response once the threat was acknowledged - was the first step in the long process that led Delta to bankruptcy today.

Develop a realistic business model once and for all

Delta's sporadic cost reduction initiatives over the last 10 years, which supposedly provided billions in annual cost "savings", have been like Chinese water torture for employees and their families. The result was many damaged lives and still an airline whose costs were so high that a bankruptcy filing was necessary.

Jerry Grinstein has commented that no airline business model is sustainable if oil continues above $50 a barrel.

With all due respect, during the first 6 months of 2005, all the low-cost carriers were profitable. America West had a small profit. Continental had a small loss. Those with the largest losses, in descending order, were United, Delta, Northwest, U.S. Airways and then American.

The message continues to be that only a truly low cost carrier can survive. Moreover, they are surviving just fine in a time of not only $50 oil, but $60 - $70 oil. Delta needs to develop a model that works for oil at this level and has a contingency plan that can be put in place immediately (not with an 8 months lead time) should oil prices go higher and stay there.

Grinstein is walking the fine line of cutting costs but keeping Delta's uniqueness, which includes employees' pride in giving good service.

Now is the time, and possibly the last one, to make the necessary decisions on a business model for Delta that respects its traditions and people but also produces a profit.

Then Grinstein will have delivered on the goal in the last sentence of his bankruptcy memorandum to employees, "Together, we will show the world a different way – the Delta way."

Insist on a sense of urgency

Delta does not have 8 months, the time taken to develop its Transformation Plan, to formulate a plan to escape from bankruptcy.

The company's destiny is, largely, in the hands of people outside the company. None is likely to tolerate long planning cycles.

As I understand the bankruptcy process, stakeholders also have the right to present their own plan to the court if it takes an excessive amount of time for the bankrupt company to present one.

Grinstein needs to set a seemingly impossible deadline for such a plan under normal circumstances and then meet the deadline.

Grinstein's words and initial actions following the bankruptcy filing indicate he understands this need for urgency. Now the sense of urgency must be sustained.

Delta's Board must step to the plate

As this book graphically demonstrates Delta's Board has missed many opportunities in its recent history to contribute to the company's health.

The Board has also contributed directly to decisions and actions that have harmed Delta's health, including the ones that have led Delta to bankruptcy.

From this point forward, Delta stakeholders have a right to expect the Board to exercise its fiduciary responsibility effectively to preserve the company and meet its commitments to its employees and others.

The Board must hold themselves and those who preceded them on the Board accountable and responsible for Delta's current situation.

The Board must also hold Jerry Grinstein accountable for his major contribution to the steps leading to bankruptcy. Part of that accountability is insisting that he remain as CEO until he has led Delta out of the woods of bankruptcy.

Board must roll up their sleeves and work

The Board also must, for the first time in recent memory, roll up their collective sleeves and make the effort to understand thoroughly what is going on inside Delta.

Getting reports from Grinstein and his team is not enough. They must proactively listen to employees and others about what is really happening inside the company, not just what management chooses the Board to hear.

Then Board members need to use proactively some of the expertise, which made them successful enough to be invited on Delta's Board, toward insuring Delta's survival and a profitable business model that retains Delta's culture.

Cutting costs is a "no brainer", as countless stories in American business over the last decade demonstrate. "Chainsaw Al" Dunlap is the poster child for that approach and the devastation that follows.

The traditional approach of bringing in a high priced management consulting firm to lead the cost cutting will no longer work at Delta.

Such firms with prior cost cutting experience say that they can "prove" the billions of dollars their clients have "saved" – the euphemism for draconian payroll cuts and cutting customer service and quality.

Of course, beginning with Leadership 7.5 and continuing with several cost cutting initiatives since then, Delta has "saved" billions, but somehow still finds itself in bankruptcy. Delta has been assisted in this futile endeavor by management consultants who have been paid millions.

Delta is 'Exhibit A' that the traditional cost-cutting approach recommended by the big management consulting firms is not right for the company, if it really is for anyone.

Had prior Delta Boards and CEOs taken the approach recommended in this book, instead of the "no brainer" one above, the book would not have been written. I doubt there would have been a need for it.

A quote in the September 19, 2005 issue of *Fortune* from GM (where Delta Chairman Jack Smith was formerly CEO) CEO Rick Wagoner seems appropriate here: "We've been around too long, and people have heard all our lies. We just have to deliver."

9 - Leadership Lessons

There are a myriad of leadership lessons throughout this book on many subjects including:

- Importance of the heart
- Values
- Attitudes
- Behavior
- Culture
- Ethics
- Integrity
- Accountability
- Expanded fiduciary role of Boards
- Long-term effect of one decision
- Long-term effect of one CEO
- Financial effects of all the above factors

The Delta story provides any leader with profound examples of how to be more effective as well as mistakes that can make a leader ineffective, so those can be avoided.

Two quotes from famous and effective leader Winston Churchill sum up the messages of this book:

"However beautiful the strategy, you should occasionally look at the results."

"Men occasionally stumble over the truth, but most pick themselves up and hurry off as if nothing happened."

I hope you have found valuable truths here.

10 – Epilogue

I am sure you will be watching with me to see what Delta's Board and Jerry Grinstein are made of.

We already know the dedication and professionalism of Delta's employees and retirees. We also know their affection toward the company and passion about it.

Now the world will see whether those ultimately responsible for Delta's health and survival – Delta's Board and CEO - can do their job and reciprocate what Delta's employees have been doing to carry out their part for decades.

Delta's low-cost, low fare competitor AirTran emerged from the ashes. The FAA decertified ValuJet, AirTran's predecessor, as an air carrier over safety issues, but it has become a successful company today.

It left the tarnished ValuJet image behind by buying smaller carrier AirTran and morphed into a respectable and growing airline. The credit for ValuJet/AirTran's survival and prosperity must be given to their leadership.

Surely, if what many considered an upstart airline can survive and prosper from their potential deathblow, Delta's Board and CEO can figure out how to survive and prosper from Delta's current circumstances.

All Delta's leaders must do is finally figure out how to cut costs and run a profitable airline, as others are doing now, while keeping Delta's unique culture.

Fuel costs won't sink Delta but leadership might.

Appendix

The following are two letters that effectively help convey messages in this book. Both writers have given me permission to reprint their letter in its entirety.

Letter 1 – Delta's Katrina response shows Delta's heart and spirit still alive even in bankruptcy

September 9, 2005 post on DP3 website

Last weekend I was unexpectedly involved with Delta in the Hurricane Katrina evacuation from New Orleans and wanted to share my experience and observations with my fellow retired Delta pilots.

Friday, Sept. 2nd, I was in the GO (Delta's General Offices) changing some of my insurance when I remembered a request that Ron Stowe (use caution when responding to requests from Ron J) posted on the DP3 website requesting volunteers to man the phones for a few hours in the Operations Control Center (OCC) to help our fellow employees affected by Katrina. Since I was in the neighborhood, I went to the OCC and was wandering around trying to find the right volunteer desk when a call came in from someone (I believe the Air Transport Association) asking if and how many aircraft Delta could provide for the evacuation. They said the commitment would be for 30 days with the government being able to cancel with a 24 hour notification.

Joe Kolshak, Tracey Bevington--the Manager of Charter Operations (I don't think she had been to bed since the original evacuation flight--24 hrs before), the Manager of the OCC and other people I didn't know conferred for about 20 seconds and then said Delta would provide six aircraft and crews. None of the people involved mentioned that we were broke or asked if Delta was going to get paid or how much---rather it was that people were hurting and Delta would help.

I told Tracey that I was a retired L-1011 pilot and part time pharmacist at Walgreens and asked if she needed help. She said she needed protective medical gear for the crews flying into New Orleans and had been having trouble trying to get the supplies. I called the District Office of Walgreens in Atlanta and told them what we needed. They called back within 5 minutes and said they would provide whatever and as much as we needed for the crews and were at that very time beginning to pull all the rubber gloves, masks and antibacterial cleansers from the shelves in several of their stores and boxing them for the flight to San Antonio. I have been blessed to have worked for two awesome companies.

Arriving in San Antonio (SAT) early Saturday morning with the crew medical supplies, I called Tracey at the OCC and asked her where she wanted them. She then told me that they had major problems with transportation because the transportation company was using their vans for FEMA and asked if I would rent a 15 passenger van and start driving. I have to admit that as I climbed in the van I thought to myself; my company may go broke, I may lose my pension and I have just put a $3,800.00 charge on my AMEX card---I am not improving my position!

Driving the evacuation transport gave me the opportunity to see and talk to a lot of the onsite Delta people sent to Texas to support the airlift. There was maintenance, ACS, charter coordinators, CSA's, ticket counter staff, ops people, station manager staff, flight crews and others that I may have forgotten. Most of the

Appendix

Delta people had been up for two days with only 1-2 hours sleep and were exhausted. There was a constant flow of Delta people between the SAT airport, Kelly AFB and the Crockett Hotel. During this time the airlift was constantly changing, as evacuation sites filled up, requiring the Delta people, although totally exhausted, to turn on a dime.

In the latter part of Saturday afternoon, the Lackland Evacuation Center (Kelly AFB) started to fill and flights began to be sent to Austin. In the early hours of Sunday, Texas decided they could not take any more people and the OCC moved to open the New Orleans to Atlanta (Dobbins ARB) air- bridge. This necessitated getting everyone up (many who had just gotten to bed after being up for two days) to board a ferry flight departing at 6:30AM to Austin to pick up the evacuation aircraft for the flights to New Orleans. The company boarded more food for the evacuees than these aircraft have probably seen in the last five years and then we were off to MSY.

Before going to Texas I had been watching a lot of the news coverage, so I thought I had a pretty good idea of what to expect in the disaster area, it wasn't anywhere close to reality. It was like trying to get your arms around hell. Even though I had spent 30 years flying into New Orleans (MSY), I had trouble picking out landmarks on our arrival because of all the water and missing buildings. The only thing that looked the same was the runway. The inside of the terminal looked like it had been sacked. It was strewn with trash and discarded personal items and it seemed like feces was everywhere because of the people being sick. There were dead bodies in the lobby waiting for refrigerated trucks. It was worse than anything I have seen in 3rd world countries when I was flying "The Flying Hospital" L-1011 aircraft, and we saw some bad stuff.

Bad as the material damage was, it didn't compare to what the people went through. When we arrived, the recovery effort was in full force with people being pulled off of rooftops and out of the water by the helicopters. The helicopters were then making parallel approaches on both sides of runway 27 and landing about every 20 seconds---the operation was massive.

After landing the people were immediately brought to the airport. After a cursory security check they were boarded on our aircraft. Probably 95% of the evacuees had never flown before. It is almost impossible to describe the terrible shape they were in. An hour before they got on our airplane, most of these people were on rooftops or in the water and many had not had food or water for up to five days. All the evacuees had a dazed look; it was like they were looking through you. One man boarded in just his boxer shorts (all he had left.) Many people were barefoot. An elderly crippled man had the bottom 12 inches broken off of his artificial leg and was hobbling trying to walk. People were boarding with dogs of various sizes--most with only a piece of rope around their neck. One 80-year-old grandmother had climbed to 3 different roof tops to be rescued.

As the people got on, they continually asked us where we were taking them. Many of the people had been separated from their families and were asking if we had any knowledge of their relatives' location and wanted to give us their phone number in case we had their family on another flight. Several of the evacuees with mental conditions, who had not had their medications for several days, were going through an additional hell. It broke everyone's heart to see any human being in this shape, let alone Americans.

Toward the end of our boarding the 2nd Delta aircraft pulled in behind us. As we taxied out through all the military traffic and took off with our load of people and animals, we resembled Noah's ark more than an airliner. It would have been appropriate for the inscription that is on the Statue of Liberty to have been painted on the side of our aircraft.

On the flight to Dobbins AFB, the smell in the cabin was almost unbearable. These poor people had been pulled from filth and had not had the opportunity to clean up. When we tried to cool the cabin down to help with the smell, people started shivering because most of them were sick and in some stage of shock. As we were dropping into Dobbins and the evacuees were looking out the window at their new home, I wondered what they were thinking.

In contrast to the confusion in MSY, the folks at Dobbins were standing tall. The governor came on board and made a short PA welcoming them to Georgia and telling them they were our new brothers and sisters and we were going to put our arms around them and help them repair their lives.

As turmoil has swirled around our airline, I had often wondered what it is like there now. As a retiree, I felt like I could walk around the tent and hear the noise, but I didn't know what was actually happening inside. Many of you have expressed the same thoughts. I have often wondered if the people still think the same way we did; do they share the same set of traditions and values we had when we worked for Delta? If I went back to work, would I recognize my company?

Lessons in Leadership

Through a fluke, I was fortunate to spend three days inside the tent interfacing with employees from a cross-section of departments, from management down. I have confidence that what I saw was the average Delta employee and not an anomaly. Let me assure you, you have done a good job of handing down the traditions and values of Delta to this 3rd generation, just as the 1st generation handed them down to us. What I saw were Delta people working, caring and giving to others---just like the old Delta I knew. I saw management committing resources, OCC people working to exhaustion (hopefully Tracey has been to bed by now), pilots waiving their contract so they could keep flying; doing whatever it takes to get the people to a safe place. ...flight attendants possibly exposing themselves to Hepatitis-A and dysentery by hugging the evacuees and helping them to walk as they boarded---while not wearing the available rubber gloves---because they did not want the evacuees to think we regarded them as aliens or outcasts.

Because of the kindness, gentleness and respect shown to the evacuees by all Delta employees, be it ground personnel, mechanics, customer service, charter coordinators or flight crews, the evacuees were being given back a sense of human dignity on their long road to recovery.

Throughout this operation, the quirky, irreverent Delta sense of humor that we all loved was alive and well and got us through some rough spots. I still chuckle when I think of Walter Goodwin (a former manager in the Atlanta Chief Pilot's Office, now a charter coordinator) looking over at me with a big grin at some point in the chaos and saying, "Mattingly, it took us 31 years, but we are finally getting some work out of you!" Gosh, I miss those times.

Appendix

Just before we took off for Dobbins, I was standing on the ramp at MSY and could not help but notice how the two tall B-757's tails carrying the bright Delta colors stood out amid a mottled sea of green, grey and brown military aircraft and debris. They must have looked like two beacons of hope to the evacuees as they boarded.

It's easier for a company to be generous and compassionate when the company is doing well and making money, but it is a true test of a company's character to offer to take care of the less fortunate when that company itself is bleeding to death and in need of life support. Standing on that New Orleans ramp and looking up at those two Delta aircraft, I experienced the same overwhelming feeling of pride in what Delta stands for as the day I first pinned a set of Delta wings on that black and gold uniform. Please know that the Delta heart - its employees--is as strong and good as ever.

In some ways we are akin to the evacuees as they face an unknown future, for we as Delta employees are also looking at uncertainty as we enter this new phase of our corporate lives -- bankruptcy. Hopefully, God will look on Delta and her people with the same compassion that we extended to the refugees in New Orleans.

I pray that God will take special care of each of you as we begin this uncharted flight!

Dave Mattingly

Captain, L-1011 (Retired)

P.S. I may be wrong but I believe that Delta operated more evacuation flights than any other airline.

Letter 2 – How Delta's leadership created the situation for which employees and retirees are now made to pay

32801 US Hwy 441 N #118

Okeechobee, FL 34972

September 27, 2005

Gerald Grinstein, Chief Executive Officer

Jim Whitehurst, Chief Operating Officer

Edward H. Bastian, Executive Vice President and Chief Financial Officer

Paul Matsen, Executive Vice President and Chief Marketing Officer

Glen W. Hauenstein, Executive Vice President and Chief of Network and Revenue Management

Joe Kolshak, Executive Vice President and Chief of Operations

Lee Macenczak, Executive Vice President and Chief of Customer Service

Board of Directors, Delta Air Lines

Hartsfield Atlanta International Airport

Atlanta, GA 30320

Sirs:

Well, here we are with Delta Air Lines in Chapter 11. And the employees and retirees are being made to sacrifice again.

Lest anyone be confused about pension plans, and what Delta owes under contract, allow me to clarify. A pension plan is part of an employee's PAY package. It is offered in LIEU of higher direct pay, in the form of a CONTRACT to pay LATER. The employee gains, supposedly, by paying lower taxes on W-2 reported income. Delta benefits by having use of the money, interest free, for years. And they are supposed to make timely payments to a fund, which they failed to do.

Retirees are creditors, just like anyone else with whom the company does business. The money is DEFERRED PAY, owed under contract.

Now, under bankruptcy, Delta seeks to pull the rug out from under retired loyal employees. We, as a group, devoted working careers to build Delta into the finest and most profitable airline in the country, and we succeeded.

C. E. Woolman, who founded Delta in 1929, considered his employees his major asset. I was told, as a new hire in 1963, that he knew all employees. I took that with a grain of salt. He came aboard a flight to Chicago one night and I met and spoke with him for all of three or four minutes. It did not click at the time that he addressed the two other pilots and the cabin crew by name. Some ten or eleven months later, I chanced across his path on the sidewalk in front of the offices. He was talking with three other men as they crossed to a waiting car. I said, "Good morning, Mr. Woolman." He turned and stepped toward me with hand extended and greeted me by NAME. He asked how I was getting along. He then asked how my wife, by NAME, was doing in her new job as secretary to the YMCA Southern Director. He chatted on as though he were in no hurry to rejoin his companions. When he finally did say goodbye, I stood stunned. My God, I thought, he really does know me and he really does care. How amazing!

That's not an earthquake; that's Mr. Woolman bouncing in his coffin over your actions.

Over the next third of a century I worked for the best company in the country, and I did it with a cheer.

Toward the end of my career, things began to erode. We got a CEO who considered that employees, especially pilots, belonged on the red ink side of his page. He would have been happier if the company could be run with no people in it. He knew only a handful of names, unless they worked on "Mahogany Row". Employees began to be seen as the root of problems, yet the first place to go for relief from costly management mistakes.

Employees and retirees are not the cause of Delta's problems. We all contributed loyally for years. How did we contribute? Well, we spent decades showing up on time and prepared to fly. We spent years in hotel rooms away from our families. We flew multitudes of passengers through thunderstorms, snow and miserable weather approaches, to their destinations. It may not sound like much, but I think it's worth something. We did our jobs. We earned our pay and retirements, as we agreed under contract.

Yet here we are again, as the first target on the wall for management seeking relief from its own mistakes. What mistakes? Some examples: We took over Western Air Lines at a time when Delta badly needed wide-body aircraft. Western owned a fleet of DC-10's and a ton of spare parts for them. But our CEO did not want DC-10's, even as a stopgap measure to increase capacity. He also did not want American Airlines to have them. So? After repainting them, he sold them for a song to a company with a proviso against leasing or selling them to American. That company sold them to another company who then sold them to American, which then proceeded to beat our brains out with them.

Then, we saw the 'let's go to the Orient' fiasco. Billions were spent on a fleet of MD-11's, despite warnings from the pilot group and many others. The MD-11 lacked the 'legs' (range) to run long non-stop routes in competition with carriers flying the B-747. But our leader argued that he could buy THREE of them for the price of TWO B-747's. What happened? The MD-11's repeatedly had to make unscheduled fuel stops in Alaska. Passengers did not appreciate the free extra take off and landing, and the re-scheduling of their connecting flights and other appointments in Japan. They defected in droves to carriers flying the B-747 and the money spent went down the drain. Where did management turn for relief? Employee pay concessions.

Then the Pan Am fiasco. Pan Am was breaking up and routes were up for grabs. What did our leader want – and get? their prestigious European routes – so he could go head to head with government subsidized biggies like KLM, Lufthansa, and British Airways. The Latin American routes were the only part of Pan Am's route structure showing a profit. We were positioned with a large pilot base in Miami, the financial HUB for South America. It is where the wealthy do business and send their kids to school, etc. But no, there's no prestige doing business with those 'Latin' people.

So, how does it end? Bob Crandall of American chivvies our leader into paying too much for the European routes, while he gobbles up the South American market. We close our Miami base and American moves in. Any guesses where a big chunk of American's black ink entries are coming from?

Then along comes the exciting new Boeing 777. Management has to have it. – at a high eight figure tag per copy. We own a fleet of beautiful Lockheed L-1011's – a real Cadillac. But they are getting old and on time departure rates are slipping due to maintenance problems. Of course, these maintenance problems have nothing to do with the forced early retirement of a cadre of experienced mechanics who know the airplane inside and out and how to fix it fast. These old beauties can be zero-timed (re-manufactured) for a few million a piece, but that would never do. "Daddy, Daddy, I don't want a nice used car – I want a new one!"

So, never mind that 95% of passengers don't know or care what model of aircraft they're on so long as they are treated well and arrive on time. Sign the papers and leap into the pit of debt. Gotta have the new toy. Never mind if we've bitten off too much. The employees will give some more wage concessions to bail us out. We can't afford to pay experienced mechanics, but we can buy another fleet of new aircraft?

Well, years of this thinking and "leadership" have finally taken their toll. Does management acknowledge any role in this failure? No. It's all due to salaries that are too high and escalating fuel costs. Gee, I never knew Delta paid more for fuel than other carriers..

So, here we are in bankruptcy court. Even now, "leadership" mistakes are not acknowledged and have no personal consequences. Management has their "golden parachutes", no personal pain. Predictably, their first target for relief is to cut wages and chop off any obligation to pay retirees those pensions WE EARNED by agreement with honorable men of the past.

This lawyer inspired abrogation of obligations is not only morally wrong, a word which appears foreign to them, but is another mistake brought about by short sighted thinking. Atlanta is a "company town." Delta's reputation, and its success, was not built by paid advertising. It was built by loyal employees talking to friends, family, and neighbors. In other words, on good will. Thousands of families will be affected by your move to cut off pensions. The ill-will and anti-Delta resentment this causes may very well be the crucial pivot which determines success or failure of any plan to resurrect Delta. Think long and hard before you shoot yourselves in the foot yet again. Northwest, in similar straits, is honoring their retirees because IT'S THE RIGHT THING TO DO.

Respectfully,

Capt. Jerry L. Farquhar, retired

With Agreement and Contributions of Retired Captains, as follows:

Capt. Thomas E. Richter, 2840 N.E. 23rd St., Pompano Beach, FL 33062

Capt. Steve Berman, 10100 SW 70th Ave., Pinecrest, FL 33156

Capt. Tom Tutton, Boothbay Harbor, ME

Buy Additional Copies

Additional copies of this book available online:

Targetmark Books™   www.targetmarkbooks.com

ISBN 0-9772076-0-9   (soft cover)

ISBN 0-9772076-1-7   (hardcover)

It is also available online at www.amazon.com

If you prefer buying in a bookstore and the book is not in stock, simply give the clerk the correct ISBN number above. Tell them to order it through Ingram, the country's largest book distributor.

Should you experience any difficulty in purchasing additional copies or to inquire about bulk purchases, please email orders@targetmarkbooks.com .

Printed in the United States
40407LVS00002B/73-108